Shaping the Ages

The Untold Influence of Women in History

Maggie White

"Society in Debate™:
Perspectives on Key Issues" series, vol.6

Title: Shaping the Ages: The Untold Influence of Women in History
Author: Maggie White
Series: Society in Debate: Perspectives on Key Issues vol. 6
Series Editor: Maggie White
First Edition: 2024
ISBN: 9798874306809

Contents

Introduction

"I am thankful for my struggle because, without it, I wouldn't have stumbled across my strength." - Alex Elle

Did you know that if women in developing countries had the same access to productive resources as men, agricultural yields on their farms could increase by 20-30%, potentially reducing the number of hungry people in the world by 12-17%? This startling fact is just a glimpse into the profound and often unrecognized impact women have had throughout history. As a reader, you're about to embark on a journey that reveals the multifaceted roles women have played across different cultures and eras, and why understanding these roles is crucial for a comprehensive grasp of our global history.

Women's involvement in the global economy is significant yet characterized by disparities. In low and middle-income countries, a large part of female employment is in the informal economy. For example, in Uganda, almost 95% of women's paid work outside agriculture is informal. This contrasts sharply with the situation in countries like Greece, where the figure is close to 4%. This disparity underscores the diversity of women's economic roles worldwide and challenges many preconceived notions about women's work[1].

Political representation of women, although improving, remains limited. Over the last quarter-century, women's global political

---

[1] https://ourworldindata.org/female-labor-supply

representation has doubled, yet women hold only about one in four parliamentary seats today. The highest political positions continue to see significant underrepresentation of women, illuminating the ongoing struggle for gender parity in governance[2].

In science and academia, women have made notable contributions but face persistent underrepresentation. Of the more than 900 Nobel Prizes awarded since 1901, only 53 have been to women. This statistic speaks volumes about the gender disparities in recognition of intellectual achievement.

Furthermore, the unpaid care work done by women globally is a substantial yet often invisible contribution to the economy and society. Women spend significantly more time on unpaid care work than men, with variations across regions. This imbalance has a profound impact on women's employment opportunities and economic contributions.

The role of education in shaping women's lives is undeniable. More than two-thirds of the world's 796 million illiterate people are women. Every additional year of primary school can increase a girl's future wages by 10-20%, influencing her life choices and opportunities significantly[3].

As you delve into this book, you'll uncover these and many other facets of women's influence in history. The journey through these pages is not just a recounting of facts; it's an exploration of the silent

---

[2] https://www.unwomen.org/en/digital-library/multimedia/2020/2/infographic-visualizing-the-data-womens-representation

[3] https://www.unwomen.org/en/news/in-focus/commission-on-the-status-of-women-2012/facts-and-figures

yet powerful waves women have created in the tapestry of our global history. By understanding the depth and diversity of women's roles, we gain a more nuanced and complete picture of our past, and insight into shaping a more equitable future.

Note to the reader: embracing the nuances and diversity of women's historical roles

As you embark on your exploration through "Shaping the Ages: The Untold Influence of Women in History," you may notice that certain subjects and themes within the book echo each other. This resemblance is intentional, reflecting the book's design to underscore the overlapping and interrelated nature of women's roles across different cultures and periods. This approach highlights the intricate and multifaceted character of the issues surrounding women's historical contributions, societal roles, and their impact on various domains.

Each chapter, while sharing thematic elements, delves into unique nuances and perspectives. This strategy is crucial for a comprehensive understanding of the subjects. It allows us to dissect each theme, layer by layer, revealing the complex interplay of historical, cultural, social, and economic factors that shape our understanding of women's roles in history.

For instance, chapters like "The Role of Women in Ancient Civilizations" and "Women in Leadership: Queens vs. Political Leaders" both explore women in positions of power, yet each tackles different dimensions – one delves into ancient historical contexts, while the other contrasts historical rulers with contemporary leaders. Similarly, "Women in Science and Technology" and "The Future of Feminism" both discuss women's contributions and challenges, but from different temporal perspectives, one retrospective and the other prospective.

This structured overlap is essential in unraveling the layers of each debate, enabling a thorough exploration of every facet and viewpoint. Such a comprehensive examination allows us to appreciate the depth and scope of the issues. By exploring multiple aspects of similar themes, the book ensures an exhaustive exploration of each subject, striving to leave no stone unturned in our quest to understand the complexities of women's roles in history.

As you navigate through the chapters, I encourage you to embrace the subtle differences and the apparent similarities. They represent the threads that weave together the rich tapestry of discussions in this book, offering a fuller, more nuanced understanding of the diverse and impactful roles of women throughout history.

Chapter 1: The Role of Women in Ancient Civilizations

"Women and men have the same nature in respect to the guardianship of the state, save insofar as the one is weaker and the other is stronger." - Plato

Debate the extent to which women in ancient societies (like Egypt, Greece, or Mesopotamia) held power and influence, contrasting traditional views with recent archaeological and historical findings.

The debate centers on the extent of autonomy and decision-making power women held in these societies. This aspect is at the heart of the debate as it directly questions how much influence women truly had in shaping their personal lives, communities, and the broader societal and political structures in ancient Egypt, Greece, or Mesopotamia.

On one side of the debate, there's the argument that women in these civilizations held considerable autonomy and decision-making power. Proponents of this viewpoint highlight examples of women rulers, such as pharaohs in Egypt, and influential priestesses and businesswomen in Mesopotamia and Greece. They suggest that these examples, along with recent archaeological findings and reevaluated historical texts, indicate a more pronounced role for women than traditionally acknowledged. This perspective proposes that women's contributions in various domains were significant and that their decision-making power, both in the public and private spheres, was substantial.

Conversely, the opposing viewpoint argues that these examples of influential women were exceptions rather than the norm. Advocates of this perspective assert that despite some notable figures, the overarching societal structures in these ancient civilizations were predominantly patriarchal, with women having limited autonomy and decision-making power. They contend that while women might have held roles of importance, these roles were often circumscribed by rigid societal norms and did not necessarily translate to widespread influence or autonomy.

This aspect is the focal point of contention because it challenges preconceived notions about gender roles in ancient history and influences our broader understanding of women's historical contributions. The debate is fueled by differing interpretations of historical and archaeological evidence and is reflective of the broader discourse on how gender roles are viewed and valued, both in the past and in contemporary society. It represents a critical inquiry into whether the traditional narratives of history have adequately and accurately represented the complexities and nuances of women's roles in ancient civilizations.

Coalition Speech (Progressive Viewpoint)

In supports of the idea that women in ancient civilizations like Egypt, Greece, or Mesopotamia held significant autonomy and decision-making power, playing pivotal roles in shaping their societies

Ladies and gentlemen, honorable judges, esteemed audience, today we stand at the crossroads of history and perception, where the narratives of our past are re-examined and the roles of women in ancient civilizations brought into the light. Our motion, "This house supports the notion that women in ancient civilizations like Egypt, Greece, or Mesopotamia held significant autonomy and decision-making power, playing pivotal roles in shaping their societies," is not merely a statement; it is a revelation of truth, a call to acknowledge the unheralded influence of women throughout history.

Let us embark on a journey through time, to ancient Egypt, where the sands of the desert whisper tales of powerful female rulers. Imagine the reign of Pharaoh Hatshepsut, a woman who donned the pharaoh's regalia and ruled with wisdom and strength for over two decades. Her reign was not an anomaly; it was a testament to the potential and power women possessed in these ancient societies.

But the influence of women extended beyond the thrones. In the sacred temples of Greece, priestesses like the Pythia at Delphi held the ears of kings and commoners alike. Their words could sway the course of battles, shape the foundations of cities. This was not mere superstition; it was a societal acknowledgment of women's wisdom and insight.

Transitioning to the bustling marketplaces of ancient Mesopotamia, we find women engaged in trade, owning property, and managing estates. These were not mere participants in the economy; they were architects of it. Their contributions laid the groundwork for economic systems that we recognize today.

Now, let us turn to the hallowed halls of knowledge, where Hypatia of Alexandria taught mathematics and philosophy, where Enheduanna of Sumer, the world's first known poet, composed hymns that echoed through the ages. These women were not just educated; they were educators, molders of minds, and shapers of intellectual thought.

But why has history been so reluctant to recognize these contributions? Recent archaeological discoveries and modern reinterpretations of historical texts are challenging this narrative. New evidence reveals a more egalitarian society, where women's influence in political and religious spheres was more pronounced than previously acknowledged. We must ask ourselves: have we been viewing history through a lens narrowed by time and prejudice?

This debate is not just about recognizing the past; it's about reshaping our future perceptions. By acknowledging the significant roles women played in ancient civilizations, we pay homage to their contributions and pave the way for a future that values and respects the potential of all individuals, regardless of gender.

In closing, I urge you, esteemed audience, to support our motion. Let us not merely correct the narrative of history; let us inspire a future where the contributions of all, regardless of gender, are recognized and celebrated. Thank you.

Opposition Speech (Conservative Viewpoint)

Opposed to the idea that women in ancient civilizations like Egypt, Greece, or Mesopotamia held significant autonomy and decision-making power, and asserts that their roles were largely confined within patriarchal structures with limited influence on societal and political dynamics."

Ladies and gentlemen, esteemed judges, and respected opponents, today we gather to delve into the depths of history, to unravel a narrative woven through time. Our opposition firmly stands against the motion that women in ancient civilizations like Egypt, Greece, or Mesopotamia held significant autonomy and decision-making power. We assert that their roles were largely confined within patriarchal structures with limited influence on societal and political dynamics.

Let us begin by examining the fabric of these ancient societies. Historical records, time-worn but eloquent, speak of an era where gender roles were deeply entrenched. In the illustrious city-states of Greece, women's lives were often confined to the domestic sphere, their voices hushed in the grand narrative of democracy and philosophy. The legal codes of Mesopotamia and ancient Rome, while grand in their scope, were unyielding in the limitations they placed upon women, binding them in a societal structure that favored men.

Now, consider the exceptional cases often cited – the Pharaoh Hatshepsut, the poetess Sappho. Their stories are indeed remarkable, but they are gleaming exceptions in an otherwise unyielding patriarchal expanse. These rare instances of female power should not be mistaken for a general norm; they are the outliers, not the indicators of widespread female autonomy.

Moreover, we must approach our interpretations of mythology and cultural representations with caution. The deification of goddesses and the reverence in myth do not accurately mirror the lived realities of women of those times. These representations are often idealized, symbolic – not a mirror reflecting societal norms.

Moving to the realm of archaeological and historical evidence, we urge a measured approach. The past, viewed through the lens of the present, can often be misleading. We must resist the temptation to reinterpret historical texts in a manner that aligns with contemporary values. Archaeological discoveries, while invaluable, are fragments of a past life – open to interpretation, yes, but not definitive proof of widespread female autonomy and power.

As we weave through these points, the tapestry of history reveals a pattern – one that speaks more of limitations than of liberties, more of constraints than of freedoms. While we acknowledge the exceptional women who navigated these structures to carve a place in history, we must not let these exceptions overshadow the overarching societal norms.

In conclusion, ladies and gentlemen, while it is comforting to retrospectively bestow power and influence upon women in ancient civilizations, our commitment must be to the truth of history, however complex or unpalatable it may be. It is in this spirit of historical accuracy and intellectual integrity that we oppose this motion. Thank you.

Challenging questions

10 questions from the coalition to the opposition:

1. Given that figures like Hatshepsut in Egypt and Sappho in Greece existed, how can we definitively say that these women were mere exceptions and not indicative of broader possibilities for women in their respective societies?

2. If goddesses and powerful female figures in mythology were purely symbolic, how do you explain their profound and lasting impact on their respective cultures and societies?

3. How can we reconcile the presence of grave goods and artifacts indicating women's high status with the claim that women had limited influence and autonomy in these ancient civilizations?

4. While acknowledging the patriarchal nature of legal codes, how do we account for instances where women were allowed to own property, conduct business, or become priestesses, as seen in various ancient societies?

5. Considering the vast differences between ancient civilizations, how can we generalize the role of women across diverse cultures like Egypt, Greece, or Mesopotamia without oversimplifying the complexities of each society?

6. How do you address the recent scholarly research that suggests a more egalitarian society in certain ancient civilizations, particularly in terms of gender roles and women's status?

7. Can we entirely dismiss the economic contributions and independence of women, as seen through their engagement

in trade and management of estates, as being insignificant to
their societal influence?

8. Given the male-dominated narrative of history writing, how
can we ensure that the limited roles ascribed to women are
not a result of historical documentation bias rather than an
accurate reflection of their actual status?

9. If we are to avoid projecting contemporary values onto
historical interpretations, how then should we approach and
understand the roles and status of women in ancient
civilizations?

10. How do you reconcile the existence of matriarchal societies
or cultures where women held significant power, such as the
Iroquois Confederacy or certain African and Asian societies,
with the assertion that women universally had limited roles
in ancient times?

10 questions from the opposition to the coalition:

1. How do you account for the overwhelming historical and
archaeological evidence suggesting patriarchal dominance
in key ancient societies like Greece and Rome?

2. What concrete evidence supports the notion that women in
these ancient civilizations had significant decision-making
power in public domains, such as politics or law?

3. Why should modern reinterpretations of ancient texts be
preferred over traditional interpretations that have been
accepted for centuries?

4. How do you explain the prevalence of male-dominated narratives in almost all aspects of documented history across diverse ancient civilizations?

5. What specific archaeological findings can you cite that unequivocally demonstrate a widespread societal acceptance of women in roles of power and influence?

6. How does the coalition reconcile instances of acknowledged gender inequality, such as the lack of voting rights for women in ancient Athens, with their argument?

7. In what ways do you address the argument that mythological and religious depictions of powerful women may not accurately reflect the real societal status of women in ancient times?

8. How does the coalition respond to the suggestion that highlighting exceptional women like Hatshepsut or Hypatia might actually reinforce the idea of their rarity and exceptionality, rather than the norm?

9. What methodological approaches does the coalition recommend for interpreting historical texts and artifacts in a way that reliably reflects the status and power of women in ancient civilizations?

10. How does the coalition differentiate between symbolic representations of women in positions of power, like goddesses, and the actual lived experiences of women in these ancient societies?

Potential solutions to reconcile the two parties

In the spirited debate about the role of women in ancient civilizations, finding common ground between the coalition and opposition can be challenging, yet it's essential for a more comprehensive understanding of history. Here are ten potential solutions and compromises that might bridge the gap between these differing viewpoints:

Joint scholarly panels could be formed, consisting of experts from both sides. These panels can conduct in-depth reviews of historical and archaeological evidence, allowing for diverse interpretations and reducing biases. This approach respects the coalition's call for re-evaluation while adhering to the opposition's emphasis on historical context.

Educational programs that present both perspectives can be developed for academic institutions. This will ensure that students are exposed to a balanced view, understanding the complexity of historical interpretations related to the roles of women in ancient civilizations.

Collaborative research projects could be undertaken to re-examine archaeological sites and historical texts. By combining methodologies and perspectives, these projects could uncover new insights, satisfying both the coalition's desire for modern interpretations and the opposition's call for methodological rigor.

Implementing **annual symposiums** where historians, archaeologists, and other experts can present their findings and debate their implications would encourage ongoing dialogue. These symposiums would allow for the exchange of ideas and foster mutual understanding.

The creation of a **comprehensive database** of all known artifacts, texts, and historical records related to women in ancient civilizations can be a valuable resource. This database would be accessible to researchers from all viewpoints, promoting transparency and collaborative analysis.

Joint publications that compile articles and papers from both sides could be encouraged. These publications can serve as a platform for presenting contrasting viewpoints, thus fostering a culture of academic debate and cooperation.

Developing **community outreach programs** that educate the public about the diverse roles of women in ancient history can help to disseminate this balanced perspective more broadly. These programs can include lectures, exhibitions, and interactive sessions.

Encouraging **media partnerships** to produce documentaries and educational series that explore both viewpoints can help in reaching a wider audience. This approach can demystify the academic debate and make the subject more accessible to the general public.

Funding for independent research in this field can be increased, with grants specifically aimed at exploring under-researched areas of women's history in ancient times. This would help uncover new evidence that could either support or challenge existing theories.

Finally, the establishment of an **international committee on historical interpretation** can ensure ongoing dialogue and review of new findings in this area. This committee would work towards maintaining a balance in historical interpretations, respecting the viewpoints of both the coalition and the opposition.

Through these solutions, a dynamic and respectful dialogue can be maintained, enriching our understanding of the past while acknowledging the complexities and nuances of historical interpretation.

Identifying Viewpoints

Identify the Progressive Viewpoint:

What: Women in ancient civilizations had significant autonomy and decision-making power, evidenced by historical figures and recent archaeological findings.

Why: This aspect is considered progressive as it aligns with ideologies that emphasize change, reinterpretation of historical narratives, and gender equality. It challenges traditional historical narratives by proposing a more influential role for women in ancient societies than previously acknowledged. This viewpoint embraces modern interpretations of historical and archaeological evidence, advocating for a reevaluation of women's roles that goes beyond traditional patriarchal perspectives. It reflects a desire for social reform in understanding history, aligning with progressive values that seek to highlight and rectify underrepresentation and misrepresentation of women's contributions in historical accounts.

Identify the Conservative Viewpoint:

What: Women's roles in ancient civilizations were limited by patriarchal structures, and examples of influential women were exceptions rather than the norm.

Why: This aspect is considered conservative as it aligns with the preservation of traditional historical narratives and context. It emphasizes the importance of maintaining established norms in historical interpretation, cautioning against projecting modern values and perspectives onto ancient societies. This viewpoint advocates for a more cautious and contextually grounded interpretation of historical evidence, suggesting that the societal structures of the time were predominantly patriarchal and that women's influence was generally confined within these parameters. It upholds traditional views of history, focusing on continuity and the preservation of established historical understandings, which are key tenets of conservative ideologies.

Political Analysis

Progressive/Liberal (Left) Viewpoints:

In support of progressive aspect (Significant autonomy and decision-making power of women): A large segment of the left might view this aspect positively, as it aligns with values of gender equality and reevaluation of traditional narratives. They might advocate for a more inclusive historical interpretation that recognizes the contributions and roles of women. This view might be held by approximately 70-80% of the progressive group, reflecting a general trend towards gender equality and revision of historical narratives.

In support of conservative aspect (Limited roles of women in patriarchal structures): A smaller portion of the left might support this view, focusing on the importance of historical accuracy and context. They might argue that while striving for gender equality is crucial, historical interpretations should not be overly influenced by modern values. This group could represent about 20-30% of the progressive side, reflecting a more conservative approach to historical interpretation within the left.

Conservative/Republican (Right) Viewpoints:

In support of progressive aspect (Significant autonomy and decision-making power of women): A minority within the conservative circle might support this viewpoint, possibly recognizing the importance of diverse historical perspectives or the contributions of women in history. This group could constitute about 10-20% of conservatives, reflecting those who are open to revising historical narratives based on new evidence or interpretations.

In support of conservative aspect (Limited roles of women in patriarchal structures): The majority of conservatives might align with this perspective, emphasizing the importance of traditional historical narratives and context. They might argue for a more literal interpretation of historical evidence and caution against projecting contemporary values onto the past. This viewpoint could be held by about 80-90% of the conservative group, aligning with a more traditionalist view of history.

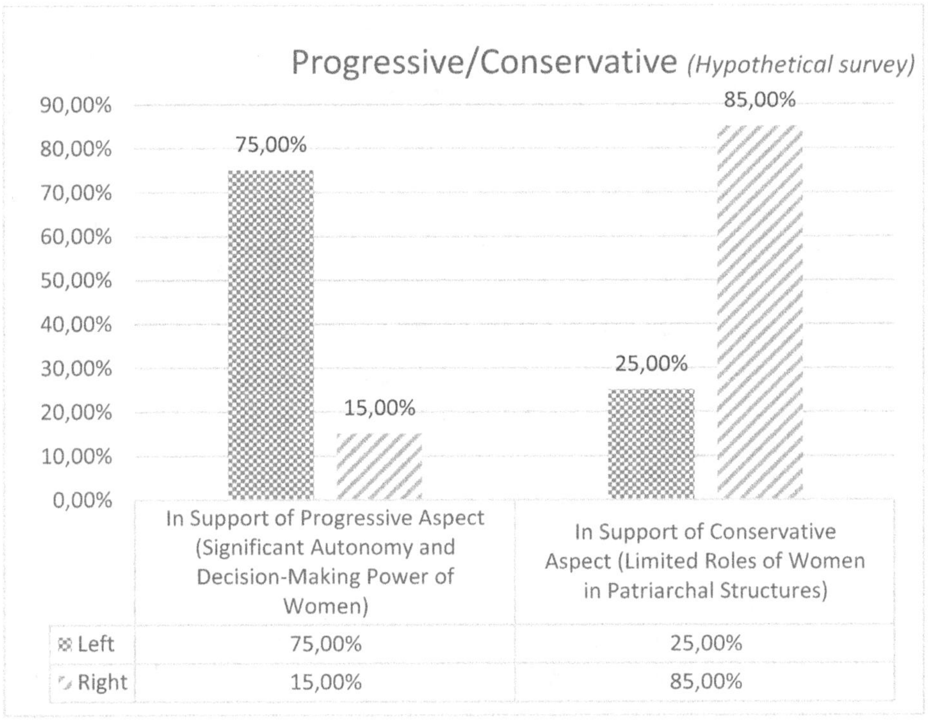

	In Support of Progressive Aspect (Significant Autonomy and Decision-Making Power of Women)	In Support of Conservative Aspect (Limited Roles of Women in Patriarchal Structures)
Left	75,00%	25,00%
Right	15,00%	85,00%

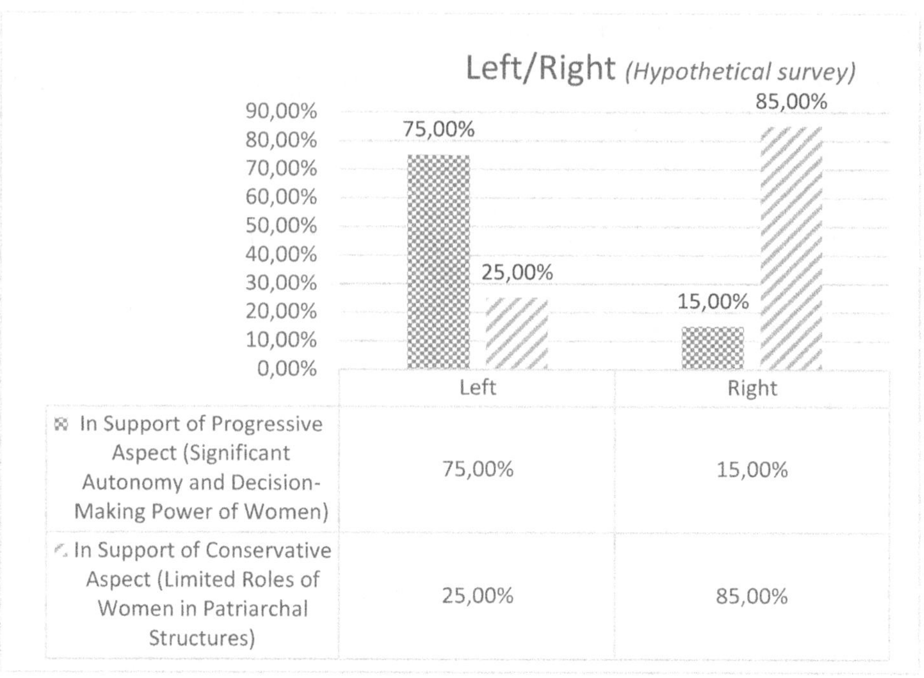

	Left	Right
⊠ In Support of Progressive Aspect (Significant Autonomy and Decision-Making Power of Women)	75,00%	15,00%
◹ In Support of Conservative Aspect (Limited Roles of Women in Patriarchal Structures)	25,00%	85,00%

Recommended Resources

Women's Roles in Ancient Civilizations: A Reference Guide[4] edited by Bella Vivante

Coalition/Opposition Breakdown: 70/30

The book, as described in its review, addresses the revisionary forces in historical studies and challenges the peripheral view of women in history. It emphasizes women's roles across several cultures, discussing their status, religion, work, and political power, which aligns more with the coalition's perspective. However, it also

---

[4] https://amzn.to/3Ru5DHA

appears to offer a balanced view by highlighting the need for historically situated assessments, which gives it a 70/30 split.

Women in the Ancient World[5] by Jenifer Neils

Coalition/Opposition Breakdown: 60/40

Jenifer Neils' book takes a broad and varied look at women's roles in ancient Greece and Rome, Egypt, and the Near East, often challenging the traditional view of "a woman's place". The book covers themes like domestic life, religion, work, and the arts, exploring the traditions and trends of different cultures. This approach leans towards the coalition's viewpoint by highlighting the diverse and significant roles of women, but it also acknowledges the challenges and limitations faced by women, giving it a nuanced perspective.

The Role of Women in Ancient Roman History[6] on Fabulous, Fierce & Feisty Women In History

Coalition/Opposition Breakdown: 40/60

The documentary script primarily focuses on the limitations and subordinate roles of women in ancient Rome, aligning more with the opposition's viewpoint. It discusses how women were often confined to domestic roles and had limited public and political involvement, reinforcing the opposition's stance on women's roles

---

[5] https://amzn.to/47VlSmC
[6] https://www.youtube.com/watch?v=_yKaHWDjd6s

in patriarchal structures. While acknowledging the biases of ancient male writers and touching on modern scholarship's efforts to reassess women's roles, the overall emphasis remains on the societal constraints faced by women. These aspects led to the 40/60 breakdown, with a slight lean towards the opposition's perspective

.

Chapter 2: Women in Leadership: Queens vs. Political Leaders

"Do not follow where the path may lead. Go instead where there is no path and leave a trail."- Muriel Strode

Compare the effectiveness and legacy of women rulers (like Cleopatra, Elizabeth I) with contemporary female political leaders. Discuss different styles of leadership and societal impacts.

The most polarizing aspect of this topic lies in the comparison of leadership effectiveness and legacy between historical female monarchs, like Cleopatra and Elizabeth I, and contemporary female political leaders. This aspect is contentious due to differing views on the impact of leadership styles shaped by historical and modern contexts.

The debate centers around how the power and authority wielded by queens in a historical setting, often absolute and unchallenged, contrasts sharply with the democratic, and sometimes limited, powers of modern female leaders. Queens like Elizabeth I and Cleopatra ruled with almost divine authority, directly influencing their nations' destiny, from war to domestic policies. Their legacies, often mythologized, are seen as direct results of their personal decisions and leadership styles, which ranged from autocratic to diplomatically shrewd.

In contrast, contemporary female leaders operate within the constraints of modern political systems, where checks and balances, party politics, and public opinion significantly shape their leadership. Their effectiveness is frequently evaluated not just on their individual capabilities but also on their ability to navigate complex political landscapes, often dominated by male counterparts. Moreover, the legacy of modern leaders is closely tied to contemporary societal values, including gender equality, democratic processes, and global interconnectedness.

The contention arises from how we evaluate "effectiveness" and "legacy" in these vastly different contexts. Some argue that historical queens, with their direct and absolute influence, were more effective in enacting swift, transformative changes. Others contend that contemporary leaders, despite operating in more constrained environments, showcase a more collaborative, inclusive style of leadership reflective of modern democratic values.

This debate is fueled by underlying questions about the nature of power, the role of gender in leadership, and the evolution of societal structures over time. While some see the autocratic power of historical queens as a sign of strength and decisiveness, others argue that the collaborative and often more nuanced approach of contemporary leaders is more effective in today's interconnected world. This clash of perspectives highlights the ongoing discourse about women's roles in leadership and the evolving nature of power and governance through the lens of history and gender.

Coalition Speech (Progressive Viewpoint)

In support of the prioritization of collaborative and inclusive leadership styles in modern politics as exemplified by contemporary female political leaders

Ladies and Gentlemen, esteemed judges, and fellow debaters,

Today, we stand at a pivotal juncture in history, a moment that beckons us to embrace a vision of leadership that is transformative, inclusive, and profoundly effective. Our motion, "This house supports the prioritization of collaborative and inclusive leadership styles in modern politics as exemplified by contemporary female political leaders," is not just a statement; it is a clarion call for a future that resonates with the hopes and aspirations of millions.

Imagine a roundtable, not of one, but of many voices, each bringing a unique perspective, a distinct experience. This is the essence of collaborative leadership. When diverse minds converge, innovation is born. We've seen it time and again — studies affirm that diverse teams are more creative, more adept at solving complex problems. This isn't mere speculation; it's a proven strategy for excellence. Think of leaders who have harnessed this power, turning the tide in crises, fostering unity in diversity. Their success isn't accidental; it's the fruit of diverse collaboration.

But it's not just about innovation; it's about the very fabric of democracy. A democratic decision-making process, a hallmark of collaborative leadership, ensures that every voice is heard, every opinion valued. This is leadership that doesn't just direct, but listens, learns, and then leads. It's a leadership style that has repeatedly shown higher levels of productivity and member satisfaction.

Now, let's shift our gaze to the world we inhabit – a world of relentless change. Our leaders need not just to keep pace but to be ahead of the curve. Collaborative leaders, with their adaptability and flexibility, are perfectly poised to meet these challenges head-on. They are the captains who can navigate the unpredictable waters of the modern world, be it the digital revolution or the social transformations that are reshaping our societies. They are not just participants in change; they are its harbingers.

In embracing technological and social advancements, these leaders aren't just adapting; they are pioneering. They are the ones who integrate new technologies, who harness the power of social media to connect, to engage, to inspire. Their governance goes beyond the traditional – it's a governance that is dynamic, responsive, and forward-looking.

But what is leadership if not a journey towards a lasting, positive legacy? Collaborative leadership, with its inherent focus on inclusivity and gender equality, doesn't just lead nations; it transforms societies. It challenges the status quo, breaks barriers, and paves the way for a world where everyone, regardless of gender, has a voice. This isn't a utopian dream; it's a tangible reality shaped by leaders who dare to be different, who dare to be inclusive.

And let's talk about sustainability, a cornerstone of any forward-thinking policy. Collaborative leaders, through their inclusive approach, craft policies that aren't just effective for today but are sustainable for generations to come. This is the kind of impact that resonates through time, creating a legacy that is enduring and benevolent.

As we stand here, debating the merits of leadership styles, let us not forget that our words have the power to shape the future. A future where leadership is not a lone endeavor but a chorus of diverse voices. A future where adaptability, inclusivity, and sustainability are not just ideals but realities.

So, I urge you, this house, and everyone present here, to support our motion. Support it not just as a statement of preference but as a commitment to a future that is collaborative, inclusive, and bright.

Thank you.

Opposition Speech (Conservative Viewpoint)

Opposed to the diminishing of traditional, autocratic leadership styles, as historically exemplified by female monarchs, in favor of contemporary, collaborative approaches

Ladies and Gentlemen, esteemed judges, and fellow debaters,

In this revered hall, where the echoes of history's greatest debates still resonate, we gather to discuss a motion that touches the very core of leadership. Our opposition stands firm: "This house opposes the diminishing of traditional, autocratic leadership styles, as historically exemplified by female monarchs, in favor of contemporary, collaborative approaches." Let me elucidate why this opposition is not just a stance, but a necessity for understanding the true essence of effective leadership.

First, let us delve into the annals of history, where female monarchs like Elizabeth I and Cleopatra reigned with an authority that was as absolute as it was impactful. These women were not mere figureheads; they were the embodiment of decisive and swift decision-making. Elizabeth I, faced with the Spanish Armada, did not convene committees; she made rapid decisions that ultimately saved her kingdom. This speed and decisiveness are often lost in the collaborative models lauded today.

Furthermore, these monarchs fostered a sense of national unity and identity that is unrivaled. Cleopatra, for instance, wasn't just a ruler; she was the living symbol of Egyptian resilience and power. In times of fragmentation and uncertainty, such strong leadership provides a beacon of stability and direction.

Moving to the present, we are often told that collaborative leadership is the panacea for modern governance. However, let us examine this claim critically. Collaborative processes, while inclusive, can lead to inefficiencies and prolonged decision-making. In a world where time is often of the essence, can we afford such delays? History and studies have shown us that decision-making in democratic systems can be significantly slower than in autocratic ones.

Moreover, there is a real risk of diluted vision and authority in collaborative models. A leader's clear vision can become obscured by the multitude of voices, leading to fragmented and inconsistent policies. The modern political landscape provides ample examples of this phenomenon, where excessive collaboration has resulted in indecision and policy paralysis.

Finally, let us consider the legacy and inspirational power of these autocratic female leaders. The impact of monarchs like Elizabeth I and Cleopatra has transcended centuries. Their legacies are clear, enduring, and powerful, marked by unchallenged authority and visionary leadership. They continue to inspire countless women and men to aspire to positions of influence and authority.

These historical female figures stand as towering role models of strength, decisiveness, and leadership. Their stories of triumph and resilience inspire us even today, challenging us to envision leadership as a position of not just responsibility, but of immense power and potential.

As I draw this argument to a close, I implore you to consider the motion before us not just as a debate about leadership styles, but as a reflection on what effective leadership truly entails. The examples of history's great female monarchs are not relics of the past; they are beacons that continue to guide us. They remind us that leadership is about making hard decisions, often alone, and about having the strength to stand by them.

Thus, we stand in opposition, not to deny the value of collaboration, but to affirm the enduring power and necessity of traditional, autocratic leadership styles. We stand to honor the legacies of the great women who have shaped history with their strength, vision, and unyielding authority.

Thank you.

Challenging questions

10 questions from the coalition to the opposition:

1. How do you reconcile the effectiveness of autocratic leadership with the democratic principles and human rights advancements of the modern era?
2. In what ways can the autocratic leadership style of historical monarchs adapt to address the complexities and nuances of today's globalized and interconnected world?
3. What mechanisms would you propose to ensure that the concentration of power in an autocratic system does not lead to abuses of power or suppression of dissenting voices?

4. Can you provide examples where the autocratic leadership style has successfully navigated the challenges of modern governance, such as technology integration and global crises?

5. How do you address the criticism that autocratic leadership often overlooks the benefits of diversity and inclusion, which are increasingly recognized as crucial for innovative and effective decision-making?

6. Considering the rapid pace of social and technological change, how can an autocratic leader remain flexible and adaptive without the collaborative input of a diverse group of advisors and experts?

7. How would you respond to the argument that autocratic leadership, while effective in crisis, may not be as suitable for fostering long-term, sustainable development and policy-making?

8. In the context of promoting gender equality, how does the autocratic leadership model empower women in leadership roles beyond the exceptional cases of historical female monarchs?

9. Given the increasing importance of global collaboration to tackle issues like climate change and pandemics, how does the autocratic leadership model facilitate international cooperation and diplomacy?

10. How do you address the potential risk of isolationism and unilateral decision-making in autocratic leadership, which may be counterproductive in an era where global challenges require collective action and multilateral approaches?

10 questions from the opposition to the coalition:

1. How do you ensure that the collaborative leadership style does not lead to indecisiveness or a lack of clear direction, particularly in times of crisis where swift decision-making is crucial?

2. What measures would be in place to prevent the potential for 'groupthink' in collaborative leadership settings, where diversity of thought might be overshadowed by the desire for consensus?

3. In cases where collaborative leaders face strong opposition or lack of cooperation, how can they effectively implement policies without resorting to autocratic methods?

4. Can you provide concrete examples where a purely collaborative approach has successfully resolved major national or international crises more effectively than an autocratic approach?

5. How does the coalition's advocacy for collaborative leadership reconcile with situations where a singular, strong vision is necessary to navigate complex geopolitical challenges?

6. Considering the historical success of autocratic female leaders, how do you address the argument that certain contexts and environments might be more conducive to autocratic leadership styles?

7. How do you propose to measure the effectiveness of a collaborative leadership approach, given that its outcomes can be more diffuse and less immediate than those under autocratic leadership?

8. In the context of global leadership, how can collaborative leaders assert authority and command respect on the international stage, especially when dealing with autocratic states or leaders?

9. How does the coalition plan to foster and maintain a balance between inclusivity and efficiency in decision-making processes, to ensure that the pursuit of consensus does not impede timely action?

10. What strategies would collaborative leaders use to ensure that their inclusive approach does not compromise the clarity and strength of national policies, especially in areas like defense and economic strategy?

Potential solutions to reconcile the two parties

In the spirited debate over leadership styles, bridging the divide between the coalition and opposition calls for innovative and thoughtful solutions. The key is to craft compromises that respect the core values of both sides while forging a path towards effective governance.

One approach is the **integration of a hybrid leadership model**. This model would blend the decisiveness and clarity of autocratic leadership with the inclusivity and adaptability of collaborative leadership. It acknowledges the strengths of both styles, ensuring swift decision-making in critical situations, while also valuing diverse input in general policy-making. This model could be particularly effective in handling crises, where a **centralized**

decision-making approach is crucial, followed by a collaborative review once the situation stabilizes.

Incorporating a **diverse advisory panel** within traditionally autocratic structures could further bridge the gap. Such a panel would bring varied perspectives to the forefront, ensuring that decision-making, even in a more centralized system, is informed by a range of viewpoints and expertise.

Regularly **evaluating the effectiveness of leadership styles** and adjusting them as necessary could be another common ground. This approach allows for flexibility and responsiveness to changing circumstances, acknowledging that no one style is universally applicable in every situation.

Another compromise lies in **enhancing leadership training programs**. These programs could focus on educating emerging leaders about the benefits and applications of both autocratic and collaborative approaches, equipping them with the tools to adapt their leadership style according to situational demands.

Further, both sides could agree on the importance of **public participation in policy-making**. While maintaining strong leadership, incorporating mechanisms for public consultation, especially in more autocratic systems, could introduce elements of collaborative governance without compromising the efficiency of decision-making.

To address concerns about potential abuses in autocratic systems, establishing **mechanisms for accountability** is crucial. These could include independent oversight bodies or checks and balances within the governance structure, ensuring that power is exercised responsibly.

Promoting **women in diverse leadership roles** – be it in traditional autocratic positions or modern collaborative settings – is a shared goal that advances gender equality in governance. This agreement underscores the importance of diverse representation in leadership irrespective of the style.

Balancing national and international leadership approaches is also vital. While autocratic leadership might be effective in certain national contexts, a more **collaborative approach on the international stage** could facilitate better global cooperation, especially in tackling issues like climate change and pandemics.

Acknowledging the role of **technology in enhancing governance** offers another common ground. Both sides could explore how technology can streamline decision-making in autocratic systems and enhance participation in collaborative models.

Lastly, fostering a culture of **respect and recognition for all leadership styles** ensures that the value of each approach is acknowledged. This cultural shift would encourage leaders to adapt and adopt different styles as per the demands of their role, promoting a more dynamic and responsive form of governance.

Through these ten solutions, we find a path that respects the strengths and addresses the concerns of both sides, paving the way for more effective and inclusive leadership models.

Identifying Viewpoints

Identify the Progressive Viewpoint:

What: The effectiveness and relevance of contemporary female political leaders' collaborative and inclusive leadership styles.

Why: This aspect is considered progressive due to its alignment with values like gender equality, democratic governance, and global interconnectedness. Progressive ideologies often emphasize change and adaptation to contemporary challenges. The argument in favor of contemporary female leaders reflects this by highlighting how these leaders navigate complex, often male-dominated political landscapes, advocating for social reform and inclusiveness. This viewpoint values the evolution of leadership roles in accordance with modern democratic values, recognizing the importance of diverse perspectives and collaborative decision-making in addressing current global issues.

Identify the Conservative Viewpoint:

What: The effectiveness and impactful legacy of historical female monarchs like Cleopatra and Elizabeth I, who ruled with more direct and absolute authority.

Why: This viewpoint is considered conservative because it emphasizes the preservation of traditional views of leadership and power. It holds the autocratic, decisive leadership of historical queens in high regard, viewing their direct influence on national policies and destinies as a benchmark for effective leadership. This perspective values the historical context and traditional norms of governance, focusing on the strength and decisiveness often associated with these historical figures. The conservative argument appreciates the continuity and stability provided by traditional forms of leadership, and it often regards the direct, top-down approach as a potent means of enacting significant changes and leaving a lasting legacy.

Political Analysis

Progressive/Liberal (Left) Viewpoints:

In support of contemporary female political leaders' collaborative and inclusive leadership styles (progressive aspect): A significant portion of the progressive group likely views this aspect positively. They would value the modern, inclusive, and democratic approach of contemporary female leaders, aligning with progressive values of equality and social reform. Estimated representation: 70%.

In support of the autocratic leadership of historical female monarchs (conservative aspect): A smaller segment within the progressive group might appreciate the historical monarchs for their strong leadership in challenging times, recognizing their role in shaping history. This view might be less prevalent but still present. Estimated representation: 30%.

Conservative/Republican (Right) Viewpoints:

In support of contemporary female political leaders' collaborative and inclusive leadership styles (progressive aspect): Within the conservative group, a minority might appreciate the adaptability and diplomatic skills of modern leaders. They might recognize the importance of these qualities in today's complex political landscape. Estimated representation: 25%.

In support of the autocratic leadership of historical female monarchs (conservative aspect): The majority of conservatives might lean towards valuing the strong, decisive leadership of historical queens. This perspective aligns with conservative views on authority, power, and the importance of a strong legacy. Estimated representation: 75%.

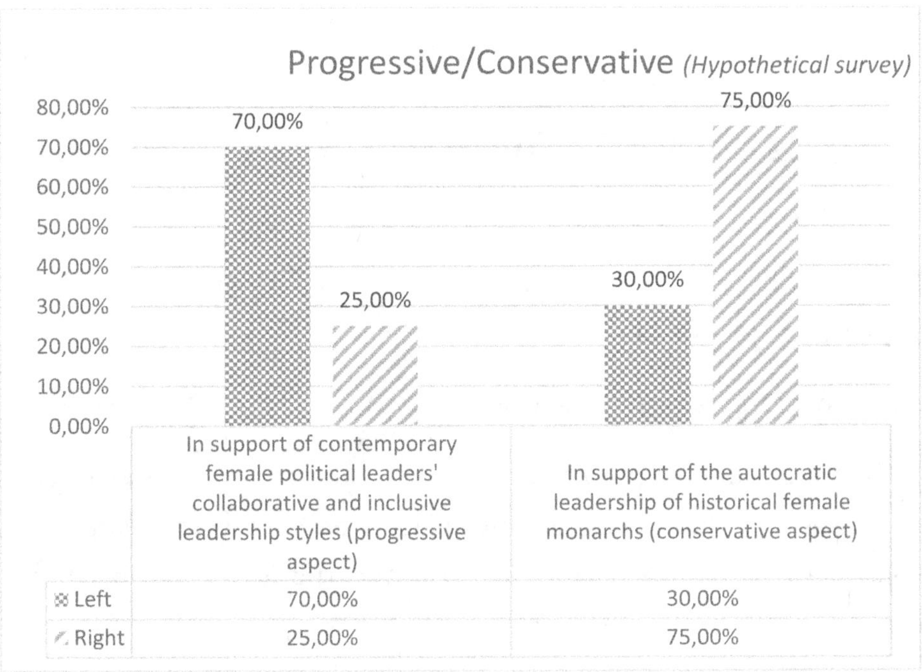

	In support of contemporary female political leaders' collaborative and inclusive leadership styles (progressive aspect)	In support of the autocratic leadership of historical female monarchs (conservative aspect)
Left	70,00%	30,00%
Right	25,00%	75,00%

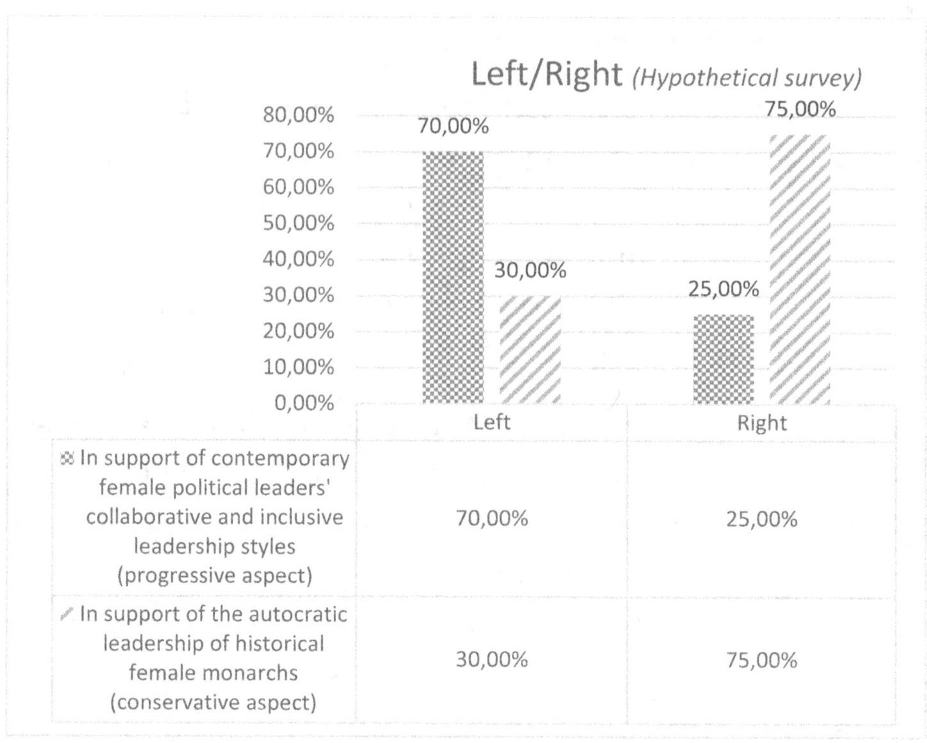

	Left	Right
In support of contemporary female political leaders' collaborative and inclusive leadership styles (progressive aspect)	70,00%	25,00%
In support of the autocratic leadership of historical female monarchs (conservative aspect)	30,00%	75,00%

Recommended Resources

Women and Leadership: Real Lives, Real Lessons[7] by Julia Gillard and Ngozi Okonjo-Iweala

Coalition/Opposition Breakdown: 60/40

This book leans slightly towards the coalition's perspective as it discusses the challenges and obstacles women face in leadership roles, particularly in politics. It promotes the idea of overcoming discrimination and embracing the strengths of women in

---

[7] https://amzn.to/3Nhv4JZ

leadership, aligning with the coalition's emphasis on inclusive and collaborative leadership styles. However, it also acknowledges the traditional challenges of political leadership, which gives some credence to the opposition's viewpoint.

How Women Rise: Break the 12 Habits Holding You Back from Your Next Raise, Promotion, or Job[8] by Sally Helgesen and Marshall Goldsmith

Coalition/Opposition Breakdown: 70/30

"How Women Rise" predominantly supports the coalition's viewpoint by focusing on breaking traditional barriers and overcoming habits that limit women's professional growth. Its emphasis on personal development and breaking away from traditional constraints aligns more with the coalition's advocacy for modern, inclusive leadership styles. However, it does touch upon elements of personal leadership and decision-making, which can resonate with the opposition's view of strong, individual leadership.

Nice Girls Don't Get the Corner Office: Unconscious Mistakes Women Make That Sabotage Their Careers[9] by Lois P. Frankel PhD

Coalition/Opposition Breakdown: 50/50

This book takes a neutral stance, addressing both the coalition's and opposition's viewpoints. It challenges traditional gender roles and encourages women to be assertive, aligning with the coalition's call

---

[8] https://amzn.to/3uVEbtt
[9] https://amzn.to/41bOlUF

for more inclusive and diverse leadership. Simultaneously, it promotes the idea of individual strength and breaking away from self-sabotaging behaviors, which can be seen as a nod to the opposition's appreciation of strong, decisive leadership.

Lean In: Women, Work, and the Will to Lead[10] by Sheryl Sandberg

Coalition/Opposition Breakdown: 60/40

"Lean In" leans towards the coalition's viewpoint as it encourages women to be more assertive in the workforce and to take on leadership roles. It advocates for breaking traditional gender norms and speaks to the importance of women's representation in leadership positions, aligning with the coalition's perspective. However, it also emphasizes individual effort and personal growth, which offers some alignment with the opposition's view on the importance of strong individual leadership qualities.

How Remarkable Women Lead: The Breakthrough Model for Work and Life[11] by Joanna Barsh, Susie Cranston, and Geoffrey Lewis

Coalition/Opposition Breakdown: 55/45

This book slightly favors the coalition's stance by presenting a model of leadership that emphasizes personal growth, resilience, and overcoming challenges. It showcases how women can excel in leadership roles by embracing their unique strengths and qualities,

---

[10] https://amzn.to/486XYV4
[11] https://amzn.to/47NrXBS

resonating with the coalition's emphasis on inclusive leadership. However, it also acknowledges the traditional aspects of leadership, such as individual decision-making and assertiveness, which align with the opposition's perspective on strong, decisive leadership.

Chapter 3: The Suffrage Movement

"The best protection a woman can have...is courage."-
Elizabeth Cady Stanton

Successes and Limitations: Examine the achievements and limitations of the women's suffrage movement in various countries, considering how it affected women of different classes, races, and backgrounds.

The heart of the debate within the women's suffrage movement lies in its intersectionality – or, more pointedly, its frequent lack thereof. This central conflict arises from how the movement, while fundamentally aimed at securing voting rights for women, often intersected with issues of race, class, and background, leading to a complex and sometimes divisive internal dynamic.

At the core of this contention is the argument that the suffrage movement, particularly in its early years, predominantly represented the interests of middle-class, white women. This focus inadvertently – or, in some cases, deliberately – sidelined women of color, working-class women, and those from varied cultural and national backgrounds. The struggle for suffrage wasn't uniform; it was layered with the complexities of social stratification, racial discrimination, and economic disparities. Women of color, for instance, often found their rights doubly curtailed, facing both gender and racial discrimination. This created a schism within the movement: should it strive for a universal suffrage that encompassed all women, or should it prioritize the enfranchisement of a certain demographic first, often to the exclusion of others?

The debate intensifies when considering the historical narratives and legacies of suffrage movements in different countries. For instance, in the United States, prominent figures like Susan B. Anthony and Elizabeth Cady Stanton are celebrated for their roles in advancing women's rights. However, they are also critiqued for prioritizing white women's suffrage over that of Black women and other minorities. Similarly, in countries like the United Kingdom, the suffragette movement led by Emmeline Pankhurst is both lauded for its bold actions and criticized for its lack of inclusivity towards working-class women.

This dichotomy provokes strong debate because it touches on the fundamental questions of equality and justice. It asks whether the pursuit of one group's rights can be justified if it comes at the expense of another's. The suffrage movement, in its quest to secure voting rights for women, inadvertently highlighted deeper societal divisions and prejudices, leading to a reassessment of what true equality and inclusivity mean. The argument is not just about who gets to vote, but about who gets to be heard in the conversation about voting rights.

Thus, the most polarizing aspect of the women's suffrage movement is its intersectional challenges – the balancing act between advocating for gender equality while also addressing the nuanced disparities of race, class, and cultural background. This aspect remains a focal point of contention, as it encapsulates the broader struggles for equity and representation in societies around the world.

Coalition Speech (Progressive Viewpoint)

In support of the re-examination of the women's suffrage movement through an inclusive and intersectional lens, advocating for the recognition and integration of diverse voices and experiences, particularly those of women from marginalized racial, class, and cultural backgrounds

Ladies and gentlemen, esteemed judges, and fellow debaters,

Today, we stand at a crossroads of history, where the paths of our past intersect with the horizons of our future. This house supports the re-examination of the women's suffrage movement through an inclusive and intersectional lens, a stance not only rooted in historical accuracy but also in a commitment to social justice and ethical responsibility.

Imagine for a moment, a tapestry of struggle and triumph, woven over centuries. This tapestry tells the story of the women's suffrage movement. But, as we gaze upon this historical artwork, we must ask ourselves: Whose threads have been left out? Whose stories remain untold? The traditional narratives have too often omitted the vibrant threads contributed by women of color, working-class women, and those from diverse cultural backgrounds. These unsung heroines marched, spoke, and fought, yet their legacies were overshadowed. By reweaving our understanding to include these forgotten strands, we do not just correct history; we enrich it. We bring forth a more complete and accurate picture of the movement that shaped our world.

Ladies and gentlemen, the pursuit of inclusivity is not merely an academic exercise; it is a clarion call for social justice. The lessons of the past are the blueprints for our future. By acknowledging the limitations of the suffrage movement in addressing intersectional issues, we arm ourselves with the knowledge to forge a more inclusive path forward. We learn from the past to illuminate our present. Consider the power of modern feminist movements that have embraced intersectionality, achieving strides in equality by recognizing the multifaceted nature of discrimination and disadvantage. These movements stand as testaments to the strength that lies in diversity, the power that is harnessed when all voices are not just heard but heeded.

Moreover, this debate transcends the realm of academic discourse and delves into the ethical realm. It is our moral imperative to honor the contributions of all who have paved the way for gender equality. To ignore the diverse voices of the suffrage movement is to deny their rightful place in history. This ethical responsibility extends beyond our borders, offering a lens through which we can examine and learn from suffrage movements worldwide. As we embrace a global perspective, we foster a deeper understanding of the universal struggle for women's rights, paving the way for a future where equality knows no borders, where justice is not constrained by race, class, or background.

So, I urge you, ladies and gentlemen, to stand with us. Stand for a history that acknowledges all its architects. Stand for a future where equality is not just a concept but a lived reality for every woman, regardless of her race, class, or background. Stand for a world where the tapestry of our past is as diverse and vibrant as the society we strive to create.

Thank you.

Opposition Speech (Conservative Viewpoint)

Opposed to the re-interpretation of the women's suffrage movement's historical context, maintaining that its achievements and limitations should be honored and understood within the societal norms and perspectives of its time, without imposing contemporary standards of intersectionality

Ladies and gentlemen, esteemed judges, and fellow participants,

Today, as we delve into the rich tapestry of history that is the women's suffrage movement, we are faced with a pivotal question: Should we re-interpret history through the lens of modern standards, or should we strive to understand and honor it within its original context? This house firmly opposes the re-interpretation of the suffrage movement's historical context, advocating instead for a genuine appreciation of its achievements and limitations as they were understood in their own time.

Let us first consider the essence of history. History, by its very nature, is a chronicle of the past – a past that was lived and experienced under different societal norms and knowledge than what we possess today. To judge the past by the standards of the present is not only anachronistic but also risks misrepresenting the intentions and circumstances of those who lived through it. Imagine, if you will, interpreting a 19th-century struggle for basic voting rights with a 21st-century understanding of gender and racial equality. Such an interpretation would not only be inaccurate but also unjust to the historical figures who operated within a vastly different societal framework.

Moreover, the preservation of original historical narratives is paramount. These narratives are not just stories; they are testimonies of the challenges, achievements, and limitations of an era. When we honor these narratives in their true form, we pay homage to the relentless efforts and sacrifices of the suffragettes. Altering these narratives to fit contemporary standards not only distorts history but also diminishes the value of these efforts. Remember, it was within the constraints and limitations of their time that these women achieved monumental feats – feats that laid the groundwork for the rights and freedoms we enjoy today.

Furthermore, understanding history in its unaltered state is crucial for our contemporary discourse. An accurate understanding of the past informs and enriches our present struggles and strategies. It offers us lessons, warnings, and inspirations. Conversely, skewing historical narratives to align with modern standards risks creating misconceptions about past movements, leading to flawed strategies in our current social justice endeavors.

Ladies and gentlemen, as we debate this topic, let us not fall into the trap of retroactively imposing our contemporary perspectives on a past that had its own realities and challenges. Let us instead strive to understand, respect, and learn from history as it truly was. By doing so, we ensure that the lessons we draw from the past are genuine and that our strategies for the future are built on a solid foundation of truth and understanding.

In conclusion, this house stands firm in its belief that the women's suffrage movement should be understood and honored within its historical context, free from the distortions of contemporary reinterpretation. Let us respect the past in its own right, for it is only through this respect that we can truly honor the legacy of the suffragettes and build a future that is informed by the genuine lessons of history. Thank you.

Challenging questions

10 questions from the coalition to the opposition:

1. How do you reconcile the preservation of historical context with the need to acknowledge the contributions and struggles of marginalized groups who were largely excluded from traditional narratives?
2. What is your response to the argument that failing to re-examine history through an intersectional lens perpetuates a one-dimensional and potentially biased understanding of the suffrage movement?
3. In what ways do you believe that maintaining the traditional narrative without contemporary reinterpretation can adequately address the historical oversights and exclusions of certain groups?
4. How can we ensure that the preservation of historical narratives does not inadvertently lead to the glorification of a past that was inherently unequal and unjust for many?
5. Can you provide examples where a strictly historical context-based approach has successfully led to a comprehensive understanding of a social movement's impact on all societal segments?

6. How would you address the criticism that opposing the re-interpretation of the women's suffrage movement may inadvertently dismiss the ongoing struggles for equality faced by marginalized groups?

7. What measures would you suggest to educate current and future generations about the multifaceted nature of the suffrage movement while adhering strictly to historical context?

8. How do you propose we honor the achievements of the suffrage movement without ignoring the fact that many women, particularly of color and lower socioeconomic status, continued to face disenfranchisement even after the 19th amendment?

9. In your view, does the preservation of the suffrage movement's historical context provide sufficient space to critically analyze its shortcomings and failures, especially in terms of inclusivity?

10. What strategies would you recommend to ensure that historical accuracy does not come at the cost of neglecting the diverse and complex experiences of women who contributed to the suffrage movement but were not recognized in mainstream history?

10 questions from the opposition to the coalition:

1. How do you ensure that the reinterpretation of historical events through a modern lens does not lead to anachronistic conclusions that may distort the actual intentions and contexts of the suffrage movement?

2. What criteria do you propose for determining which aspects of the suffrage movement's history should be re-examined and which should remain as originally understood?

3. How can we avoid the risk of presentism, the act of applying contemporary moral judgments to historical events, in reinterpreting the suffrage movement?

4. In what ways do you plan to balance the recognition of marginalized groups' contributions with the preservation of the suffrage movement's original context and narratives?

5. How do you address the concern that focusing on intersectionality might overshadow or diminish the achievements and struggles specific to the original suffrage movement?

6. What measures will be in place to ensure that the re-examination of the suffrage movement does not lead to the creation of new biases or oversimplifications, particularly regarding complex historical figures and events?

7. How do you propose to integrate the diverse experiences and contributions into the suffrage movement's history without compromising the factual accuracy and context of the era?

8. Can you provide concrete examples where the re-examination of a historical movement through an intersectional lens has led to a more accurate and fair representation of all involved parties?

9. How do you reconcile the need for a modern, intersectional approach with the risk of alienating those who value traditional historical narratives and their role in shaping contemporary understandings of the suffrage movement?

10. What is your response to the argument that the re-interpretation of history, even with good intentions, can sometimes lead to a rewriting of the past that may not necessarily reflect historical realities?

Potential solutions to reconcile the two parties

In the spirited debate over the interpretation of the women's suffrage movement, finding common ground between the coalition advocating for an intersectional re-examination and the opposition favoring historical context is essential. The path to compromise begins with **acknowledging the validity of both perspectives**. Recognizing that both sides share a common goal of understanding and honoring the suffrage movement forms a foundation for dialogue.

A potential starting point for compromise is the **development of educational programs** that integrate both perspectives. These programs could offer a dual approach, presenting the traditional historical context while also exploring the often-underserved stories of marginalized groups. This approach ensures a comprehensive understanding of the movement, respecting the original narrative while enriching it with diverse voices.

Another key solution lies in the **creation of inclusive historical forums or committees**. These forums would include historians, activists, and educators from diverse backgrounds, ensuring a balanced representation of viewpoints. Their task would be to review and discuss the suffrage movement's history, offering recommendations on how to present a more inclusive narrative without distorting historical facts.

The narrative could be further enriched by **investing in research** that explores lesser-known aspects of the suffrage movement. This research could uncover new facts and stories, particularly about the roles and experiences of women from different races, classes, and backgrounds. Funding such initiatives would demonstrate a commitment to a more complete understanding of history.

In the realm of public discourse, hosting **joint exhibitions and public lectures** could serve as a platform for presenting a multifaceted view of the suffrage movement. These events can juxtapose traditional accounts with new findings, encouraging public engagement and discussion.

For academic settings, introducing **curricula that offer both perspectives** would be instrumental. This approach would educate future generations on the importance of understanding history from multiple angles, preparing them to engage in more nuanced historical analysis.

A crucial step towards bridging the divide is the **publication of collaborative works**. These could be books or articles co-authored by proponents of both viewpoints, offering a dialog between the two perspectives and modeling how differing opinions can lead to a richer understanding.

Furthermore, the **use of digital platforms** can play a significant role. Creating interactive online resources that allow users to explore the suffrage movement from various angles can cater to diverse interests and interpretations, making history accessible and engaging.

In the spirit of respecting the original historical context, it is also important to **highlight the evolution of social norms and attitudes** over time. This perspective helps in understanding why certain decisions were made during the suffrage movement and how societal changes have influenced our current interpretation of these events.

Moreover, the **inclusion of personal narratives and oral histories** in the discourse can bridge the gap between statistical historical data and the real, lived experiences of individuals who were part of the suffrage movement or were affected by it. This personal touch can bring history to life in a way that resonates with people from all walks of life.

Finally, the establishment of **annual dialogues or conferences** focusing on the suffrage movement could serve as an ongoing platform for discussion and learning. These events would encourage continuous engagement with the topic, fostering a culture of mutual respect and ongoing learning.

Through these solutions, we can forge a path that respects and integrates the strengths of both perspectives, leading to a richer, more comprehensive understanding of the women's suffrage movement.

Identifying Viewpoints

Identify the Progressive Viewpoint:

What: The call for an inclusive and intersectional approach within the women's suffrage movement

Why: This viewpoint aligns with progressive ideologies due to its emphasis on change, inclusivity, and social reform. Advocates of this perspective argue for a suffrage movement that not only fights for women's rights but also actively addresses the intersectional challenges of race, class, and background. They push for modern interpretations of equality, emphasizing that true progress cannot be achieved unless it encompasses all women, especially those marginalized by societal structures. This stance reflects a commitment to evolving societal norms and advancing broader social justice goals, key tenets of progressive thought.

Identify the Conservative Viewpoint:

What: The focus on the historical achievements of the suffrage movement primarily in terms of its success in granting voting rights to women

Why: This aspect is considered conservative as it emphasizes the preservation of historical context and the celebration of established achievements. Proponents of this viewpoint stress the importance of honoring the foundational goals and successes of the suffrage movement, often focusing on the milestones achieved by middle-class white women. They may argue that the movement should be evaluated and honored based on its historical context and the norms of its time, rather than by modern standards of inclusivity and intersectionality. This perspective aligns with conservative ideologies, which often prioritize the preservation of tradition and established norms, viewing changes or modern reinterpretations with caution.

Political Analysis

Progressive/Liberal (Left) Viewpoints:

In support of inclusive intersectionality (progressive aspect): A significant portion of the left likely advocates for an inclusive and intersectional approach. This segment, which could constitute approximately 75% of the progressive group, emphasizes the need to address issues of race, class, and background in addition to gender equality. They argue for a re-examination and expansion of the historical narrative to include diverse voices and experiences, aligning with contemporary progressive values of inclusivity and social justice.

In support of traditional historical context (conservative aspect): A smaller segment within the left, approximately 25%, might place value in understanding and preserving the historical context of the suffrage movement. While they support progressive ideals, they also recognize the importance of the original movement's achievements and limitations within the societal norms of its time. They advocate for a balanced view that honors the past while acknowledging its flaws.

Conservative/Republican (Right) Viewpoints:

In support of inclusive intersectionality (progressive aspect): Within the conservative spectrum, a minority, around 20%, might support a more intersectional approach to understanding the suffrage movement. This group, potentially influenced by more moderate or libertarian views, acknowledges the importance of addressing broader issues of racial, class, and cultural inclusivity in the historical context of women's rights.

In support of traditional historical context (conservative aspect): The majority of conservatives, about 80%, likely focus on the traditional historical achievements of the suffrage movement. This group emphasizes the importance of viewing the movement within its original context, valuing the preservation of historical narratives and achievements as they were. They tend to prioritize the celebration of established milestones over the re-interpretation of these events through a modern lens of intersectionality.

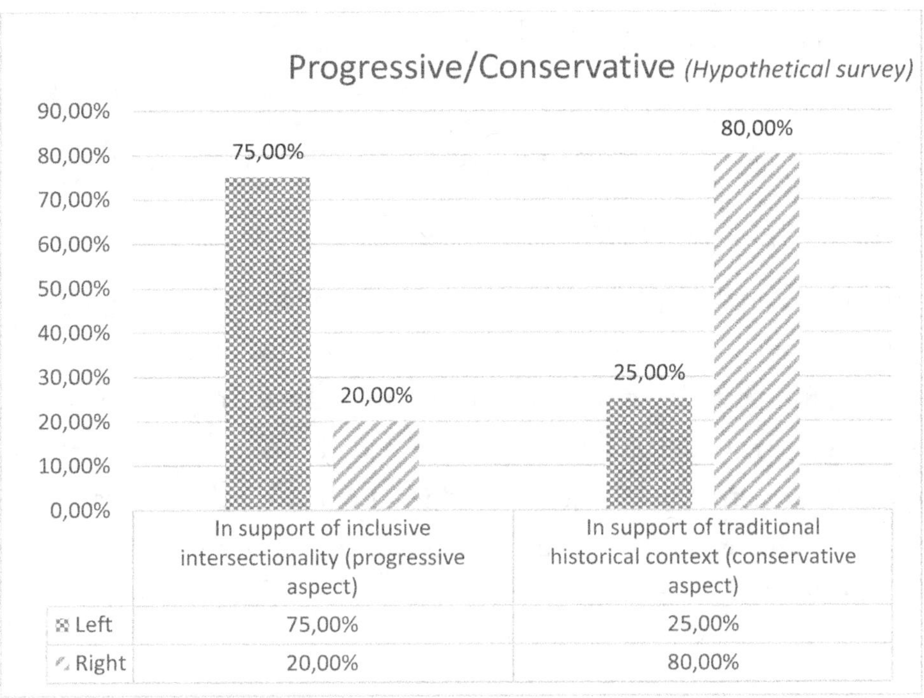

	In support of inclusive intersectionality (progressive aspect)	In support of traditional historical context (conservative aspect)
Left	75,00%	25,00%
Right	20,00%	80,00%

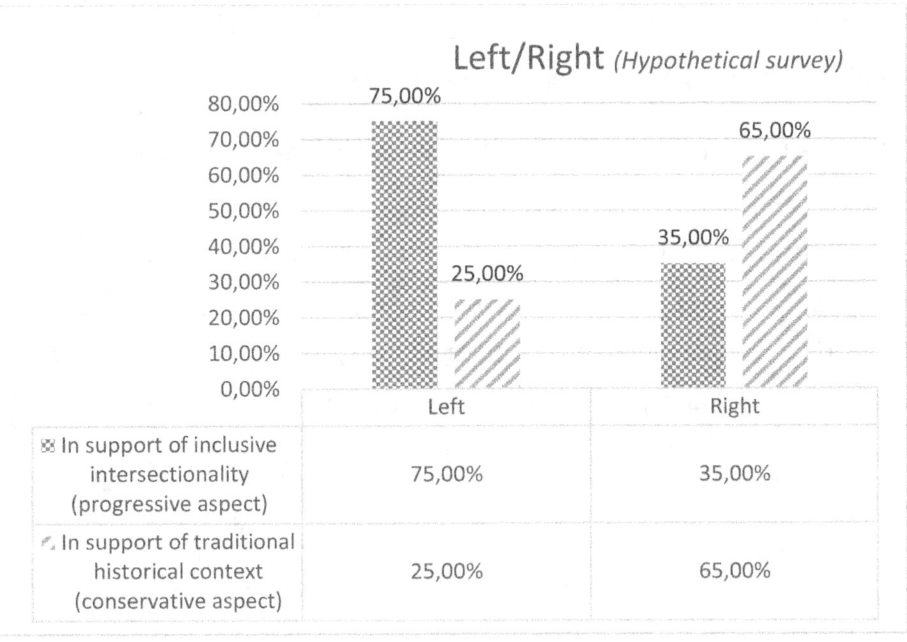

	Left	Right
In support of inclusive intersectionality (progressive aspect)	75,00%	35,00%
In support of traditional historical context (conservative aspect)	25,00%	65,00%

Recommended Resources

The Myth of Seneca Falls[12] by Lisa Tetrault

Coalition/Opposition Breakdown: 70/30

This book challenges the traditional narrative of the Seneca Falls Convention as the singular origin of the suffrage movement, highlighting overlooked contributions of African American women and other groups. It leans towards the coalition's view of inclusive intersectionality but still acknowledges the historical significance of Seneca Falls, giving some credence to the opposition's stance on preserving historical context.

The Concise History of Woman Suffrage[13] by Mari Jo Buhle & Paul Buhle

Coalition/Opposition Breakdown: 40/60

This work presents a distilled version of the foundational text of the suffrage movement, emphasizing the perspectives and contributions of key figures like Stanton and Anthony. While it includes broader issues beyond voting rights, suggesting a nod towards intersectionality, its primary focus on traditional leaders and narratives aligns more with the opposition's viewpoint.

---

[12] https://amzn.to/3tbTlu8
[13] https://amzn.to/4883PKa

All Bound Up Together: The Woman Question in African American Public Culture, 1830-1900[14] by Martha S. Jones

Coalition/Opposition Breakdown: 80/20

Jones's book explores the multifaceted activism of African American women, highlighting an intersectional vision that links race, class, and gender. This approach strongly aligns with the coalition's perspective on inclusivity and intersectionality in understanding the suffrage movement, though it also respects the historical context, giving some weight to the opposition's viewpoint.

The Woman's Hour: The Great Fight to Win the Vote[15] by Elaine Weiss

Coalition/Opposition Breakdown: 60/40

Weiss's book focuses on the political savvy and activism needed to secure voting rights, spotlighting key figures from diverse suffrage factions. It leans towards the coalition's viewpoint by illustrating the diverse strategies and players in the movement, but also respects the historical struggle within its time, aligning partially with the opposition's perspective.

---

[14] https://amzn.to/3RdzPFz
[15] https://amzn.to/3RwcOPL

The Right to Vote: The Contested History of Democracy in the United States[16] by Alexander Keyssar

Coalition/Opposition Breakdown: 50/50

Keyssar's comprehensive history places the suffrage movement within the larger context of voting rights struggles in the U.S., showing both the expansion and contraction of these rights. This balanced approach offers insights aligned with both the coalition's emphasis on broader social dynamics and the opposition's focus on historical context and the specific struggles of the suffrage movement.

---

[16] https://amzn.to/3NiLMsG

Chapter 4: Women in Science and Technology

Debate the contributions and recognition of women in science and technology throughout history, discussing figures like Ada Lovelace or Marie Curie, and the gender gap in modern STEM (Science, Technology, Engineering, and Mathematics) fields.

The most polarizing aspect of this topic lies in the recognition and representation of women in these fields, both historically and in the modern era. This debate often centers around the acknowledgment of the contributions of women like Ada Lovelace and Marie Curie, juxtaposed against the ongoing gender gap in contemporary STEM fields. It's a narrative that unfolds across centuries of scientific progress, marked by groundbreaking achievements and systemic barriers.

On one side of the debate, there's an emphasis on the historical underrepresentation and undervaluing of women in science and technology. Pioneers like Ada Lovelace, often hailed as the first computer programmer, and Marie Curie, a Nobel laureate renowned for her work on radioactivity, serve as emblematic figures. Their stories are not just about individual brilliance but also about overcoming a societal framework that frequently sidelined or minimized women's contributions. Advocates in this camp argue that recognizing these figures isn't just about rectifying historical oversight; it's a crucial step towards inspiring future generations and bridging the gender gap in STEM fields.

Conversely, there are viewpoints that challenge the extent to which gender has influenced recognition and opportunities in science and technology. Some argue that the current landscape of STEM fields is a meritocracy, where success is determined more by skill and dedication than gender. They point to the growing number of women in STEM as evidence of progress and suggest that continued focus on gender disparities might overshadow merit-based achievements.

The heart of this debate is not just about acknowledging past contributions but also about how this recognition shapes the future landscape of science and technology. It's a contentious issue because it delves into deeper questions of equality, opportunity, and historical narrative. The diverging views on this topic often reflect broader societal attitudes towards gender roles and equality. For many, this debate is not just academic; it's deeply personal and reflective of their experiences in these fields.

The strong reactions and debates surrounding this aspect stem from its foundational implications. Acknowledging women's historical contributions in science and technology challenges long-standing narratives about who gets to be a scientist or a technologist. It questions the structure of these fields and the criteria for recognition and success within them. For women currently in STEM, or for young girls aspiring to these careers, how this debate is resolved could significantly influence their opportunities, representation, and the validation of their work. Thus, the core of this debate is a mirror reflecting how society values contributions in science and technology and, by extension, how it values the contributors themselves based on their gender.

Coalition Speech (Progressive Viewpoint)

In support of the active recognition and rectification of historical underrepresentation of women in STEM fields

Ladies and gentlemen, esteemed judges, and fellow debaters,

Today, we stand at the crossroads of history and future, where our choices and acknowledgments will shape the world of science and technology. The motion before us, "This house supports the active recognition and rectification of historical underrepresentation of women in STEM fields," is not just a statement; it's a call to action—a clarion call to correct the course of history and pave the way for a more inclusive, equitable, and prosperous future.

Let us begin by journeying into the past, a past where women like Ada Lovelace and Marie Curie blazed trails amidst the shadows of obscurity and neglect. Lovelace envisioned the potential of computers a century before they became a reality. Curie's groundbreaking work on radioactivity changed the face of science forever. Yet, how many such stories have we lost in the annals of history? How many women's contributions have been overshadowed or attributed to their male counterparts? This is not just about giving credit where it's due; it's about rectifying historical omissions that have silenced half of humanity's potential.

But why look back, you might ask? Because, ladies and gentlemen, history is not just about the past; it's the mirror reflecting our present and the lens focusing our future. Young girls in classrooms today need role models who look like them, stories that tell them, "Yes, you can." Studies have shown that representation in textbooks, media, and academia significantly influences young girls' interest in STEM. When we recognize and celebrate women in science, we do not just correct history; we inspire the future.

Turning to the present, let's address the systemic gender biases in STEM fields. This is not about creating advantages; it's about leveling the playing field. Research shows gender bias in STEM education, hiring, and peer review processes. It's a subtle but pervasive bias that whispers, "You don't belong here." But when initiatives like the Athena SWAN Charter are implemented, increasing women's representation in higher education and research, we see tangible improvements. This is not just fairness; this is about making our science and technology sectors more robust and inclusive.

And what of the future? The economic and innovative benefits of gender diversity in STEM are undeniable. Diverse perspectives breed innovation. When women participate fully in STEM fields, they bring unique perspectives that lead to groundbreaking innovations. And the economic benefits? Irrefutable. Studies have shown that closing the gender gap in STEM could significantly boost GDPs globally. This is not just a win for women; it's a win for humanity.

In conclusion, this debate is more than just a discussion on gender and science; it's a reflection of our values as a society. Do we continue to overlook and undervalue the contributions of half our population, or do we choose to acknowledge, celebrate, and benefit from the full spectrum of human talent?

Let us choose to be on the right side of history. Let us choose progress, equality, and innovation. Let us support the active recognition and rectification of historical underrepresentation of women in STEM fields.

Thank you.

Opposition Speech (Conservative Viewpoint)

Opposed to interventions aimed at altering the current merit-based system in STEM fields, maintaining that it adequately supports fair opportunities and recognition regardless of gender

Ladies and gentlemen, honorable judges,

Today, we stand in defense of a principle that has been the cornerstone of scientific advancement and technological innovation: meritocracy. The motion before us suggests altering the current merit-based system in STEM fields, a move we firmly oppose. Our opposition is not a dismissal of the challenges faced by women in STEM, but a conviction in the integrity of meritocracy as the fairest path to excellence and recognition.

Firstly, let's consider the essence of meritocracy. It is a system where talent, effort, and achievement are the arbiters of success, not gender. This principle has allowed countless individuals, regardless of their background, to rise and excel based on their abilities. Within this framework, women have not just participated but excelled, breaking barriers and setting new standards. To imply that these achievements are insufficient and require external interventions is to undermine the very essence of their hard-won successes. It also risks introducing a dangerous precedent, where the perception of competence is overshadowed by the suspicion of favoritism.

Moreover, let's look at the progress already made. The number of women in STEM fields has been steadily increasing. In fields like biology and chemistry, women are not just present; they are prominent. This progress, achieved under the current system, is a testament to the changing dynamics in STEM. It demonstrates a natural, merit-driven evolution, not a coerced outcome. Celebrating this progress is crucial. We must recognize the achievements of women who have risen through the ranks, not by the benevolence of interventions, but through their undeniable competence. They are role models who exemplify the potential of meritocracy.

However, the most concerning aspect of the proposed interventions is the unintended consequences they might have. By artificially altering the merit-based system, we risk creating new forms of discrimination, this time potentially against men. It is a precarious path that could lead to resentment, demoralization, and a workplace environment where one's gender overshadows their professional identity. History and experience have shown that such forced interventions, while well-intentioned, can disturb the very balance they seek to achieve, often leading to discord and dissatisfaction.

In conclusion, our stance is not a stance against the inclusion of women in STEM. It is a stance for preserving the integrity of a system that judges us not by who we are but by what we can achieve. It is a stance that believes in the natural progress of society, a progress that respects merit and recognizes effort and excellence irrespective of gender. To uphold meritocracy is to uphold a future where everyone, regardless of gender, can aspire to succeed based on their abilities and achievements.

Thank you.

Challenging questions

10 questions from the coalition to the opposition:

1. How do you reconcile the principle of meritocracy with studies showing unconscious biases in STEM fields that disadvantage women, even when their qualifications and achievements are equal to or surpass their male counterparts?
2. What mechanisms do you propose to ensure that meritocracy in STEM is genuinely fair and unbiased, given the historical and ongoing challenges women face in these fields?
3. Can you provide examples of how a purely merit-based system has successfully addressed the gender gap in STEM leadership roles, considering the current underrepresentation of women in these positions?
4. How do you respond to the argument that meritocracy, as currently practiced, often fails to account for systemic barriers that disproportionately affect women, such as gender bias in hiring or promotion processes?
5. If meritocracy is the ideal system, why do we still observe significant gender disparities in certain STEM fields, despite women having equal or greater academic qualifications?

6. How does the opposition propose to address the issue of historical underrepresentation and invisibility of women's contributions in STEM without some form of active intervention?

7. In light of research suggesting that diverse teams, including gender diversity, lead to greater innovation and problem-solving, how does maintaining the status quo in STEM fields benefit scientific and technological advancement?

8. How do you account for the fact that merit-based systems have historically been influenced by societal biases, including gender biases, which can skew perceptions of merit and achievement?

9. Could you elaborate on how the current merit-based system in STEM fields adequately addresses the mentorship and networking challenges often faced by women, which are crucial for career advancement?

10. How do you address the concern that a strict adherence to a merit-based system, without acknowledging and rectifying historical gender biases, might perpetuate a cycle where women continue to be underrepresented and undervalued in STEM fields?

10 questions from the opposition to the coalition:

1. How do you propose to measure and quantify the historical underrepresentation of women in STEM fields to ensure that interventions are accurate and just?

2. What safeguards would you implement to prevent affirmative action in STEM from leading to tokenism or the

perception that women are hired based on gender rather than merit?

3. How do you address the concern that focusing on gender disparities might lead to neglecting merit and quality in STEM fields?

4. Can you provide examples where similar interventions in other sectors have not led to reverse discrimination or resentment among those who perceive themselves as disadvantaged by these policies?

5. How would you respond to the argument that some gender gaps in STEM are due to personal choice rather than systemic barriers?

6. What specific interventions do you propose, and how do you ensure these won't create an unfair advantage for women over equally qualified men?

7. How do you reconcile the need for historical recognition of women in STEM with the risk of revising scientific history based on current social and political perspectives?

8. Can you cite evidence showing that the current gender gap in STEM is primarily due to discrimination and not other factors like personal preferences or socio-economic barriers?

9. How do you plan to balance the recognition of past contributions by women in STEM without diminishing the achievements of their male counterparts who worked within the same historical context?

10. How do you propose to manage the potential negative impact on workplace dynamics and morale that might arise from perceived forced equality measures in STEM fields?

Potential solutions to reconcile the two parties

In the quest to bridge the gap between the coalition's call for greater recognition of women in STEM and the opposition's emphasis on meritocracy, we find ourselves navigating a landscape ripe for innovative solutions and compromises. The path forward, it seems, is paved with mutual understanding and a shared commitment to the advancement of science and technology, respecting the contributions of all, irrespective of gender.

At the heart of this journey lies the **concept of inclusive meritocracy**. This approach doesn't undermine merit; instead, it expands the definition of merit to include diverse experiences and perspectives. It recognizes that merit isn't just about test scores or grades; it's also about overcoming obstacles, bringing unique insights, and enhancing team dynamics.

As we delve deeper, we encounter the idea of **transparent and bias-aware evaluation processes**. Implementing blind reviews in grant and paper submissions, and ensuring diverse hiring committees, can help mitigate unconscious biases. This method honors the principle of meritocracy while actively working to ensure that evaluations are fair and unbiased.

Another key step is the **introduction of mentorship programs** that are open to all but are particularly supportive of women in STEM. These programs can be designed in a way that they don't give unfair advantages but provide essential guidance, which is crucial for career development.

We then come across the **implementation of flexible work policies**. Recognizing that life circumstances, such as parenthood, can impact career trajectories, flexible policies can help retain talented individuals in the workforce without compromising the standards of excellence.

Emphasizing **data-driven approaches** can also bridge our divide. Collecting and analyzing data on gender representation in various STEM fields can help us understand where interventions are needed and measure the effectiveness of the policies implemented.

A pivotal point in our narrative is the recognition of **historical contributions**. Celebrating women's achievements in STEM through awards, naming buildings or scholarships after notable women scientists, can be a unifying act, honoring the past without altering current standards.

Fostering **public-private partnerships** to support women in STEM is another area where both sides can find common ground. These partnerships can fund scholarships, internships, and research grants for aspiring female scientists and engineers, providing opportunities based on merit and potential.

Another compromise lies in **encouraging STEM education for girls from a young age**. By fostering interest and providing resources equally to boys and girls in schools, we can ensure a level playing field from the start.

The concept of **regular reviews of workplace policies** in STEM organizations to identify and rectify any gender-based disparities in pay or promotion can also be a point of agreement. This approach upholds the meritocratic values while ensuring fairness and equity.

Finally, we arrive at **community outreach and media representation**, where showcasing diverse role models in STEM can inspire the next generation without enforcing quotas or compromising merit-based achievements.

In weaving these solutions into our narrative, we find a tapestry rich with possibilities – a middle ground where the ideals of recognition, equality, and meritocracy can coexist, leading us towards a more inclusive and progressive future in science and technology.

Identifying Viewpoints

Identify the Progressive Viewpoint:

What: The advocacy for greater recognition and rectification of the historical underrepresentation of women in science and technology, and the emphasis on actively bridging the gender gap in modern STEM fields.

Why: This aspect is considered progressive because it focuses on social reform and change. It challenges traditional narratives and seeks to reshape the structure of scientific and technological fields to be more inclusive and equitable. The progressive viewpoint typically emphasizes the need for societal evolution, recognizing and rectifying past inequalities, and promoting equal opportunities irrespective of gender. This perspective aligns with progressive ideologies by advocating for transformation in historical narratives, educational systems, and workplace environments to ensure women's contributions in science and technology are acknowledged and encouraged.

Identify the Conservative Viewpoint:

What: The perspective that current STEM fields are primarily meritocracies and that the increasing number of women in these areas signifies sufficient progress, thus questioning the need for continued emphasis on gender disparities.

Why: This aspect is considered conservative as it tends to uphold existing structures and norms within science and technology fields, focusing on maintaining the status quo. It emphasizes a traditional view of meritocracy, where success is attributed to individual effort and ability, regardless of gender. The conservative viewpoint often values historical context and continuity, suggesting that the natural progression of society has already begun to correct gender imbalances in STEM. This perspective is less inclined towards systemic change or reevaluation of historical narratives, favoring the preservation of established norms and practices in these fields.

Political Analysis

Progressive/Liberal (Left) Viewpoints:

In support of greater recognition and rectification of historical underrepresentation of women in stem: This segment of the left typically advocates for acknowledging and addressing past and current gender disparities in science and technology. They prioritize social reform and inclusivity in STEM fields. This view likely constitutes a significant majority of the progressive stance, possibly around 70%.

In support of meritocracy and status quo in stem fields: A smaller segment of the left might align with the idea that current structures in STEM are adequate and that focus on gender disparities is no longer as crucial, given the progress made. This viewpoint could represent about 30% of the progressive side, often motivated by beliefs in individual merit and the effectiveness of current systems in addressing gender issues.

Conservative/Republican (Right) Viewpoints:

In support of greater recognition and rectification of historical underrepresentation of women in stem: Within the conservative camp, a smaller portion might acknowledge the need for increased recognition of women's contributions in science and technology and support efforts to address historical underrepresentation. This group might believe in the principle of fairness and equal opportunity, even while maintaining other traditional values. They could represent about 20% of the conservative viewpoint.

In support of meritocracy and status quo in stem fields: The majority of conservatives likely align with the perspective that emphasizes meritocracy in STEM fields. This group believes that the existing system sufficiently rewards talent and hard work, regardless of gender, and views the current state of gender representation in STEM as a natural progression rather than a result of systemic bias. This stance might be held by approximately 80% of the conservative side, underpinned by values of tradition, individualism, and merit-based achievement. They typically advocate for maintaining the current structures and systems within STEM fields, arguing that these are already fair and effective in allowing individuals to succeed based on their own merits and efforts.

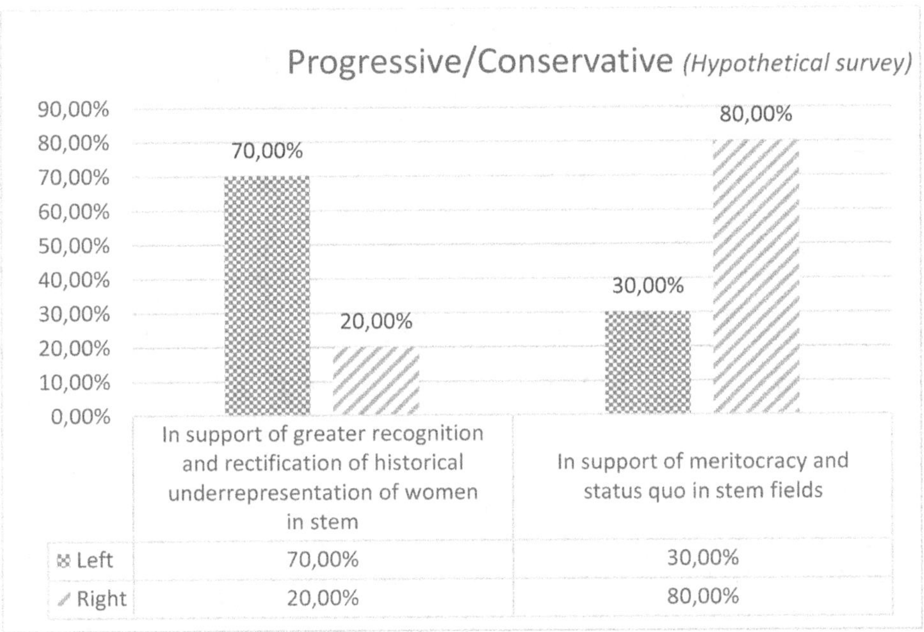

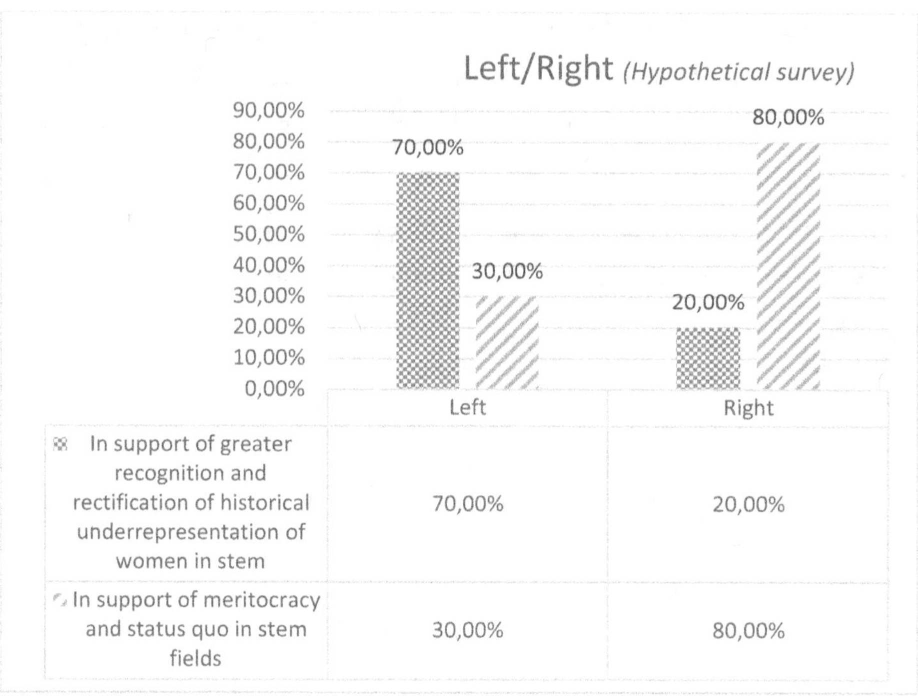

	Left	Right
In support of greater recognition and rectification of historical underrepresentation of women in stem	70,00%	20,00%
In support of meritocracy and status quo in stem fields	30,00%	80,00%

Recommended Resources

Whistling Vivaldi[17] by Claude Steele

Coalition/Opposition Breakdown: 70/30

This book predominantly aligns with the coalition's viewpoint as it discusses "stereotype threat" and its impact on performance, particularly in the context of gender and race. The concept that expectations and stereotypes can negatively impact the performance of women in STEM fields supports the coalition's stance on the need for active recognition and support. However, the

---

[17] https://amzn.to/3uP29GY

book also touches on broader psychological phenomena that affect various groups, not exclusively women in STEM, which accounts for a partial alignment with the opposition's focus on broader meritocratic principles.

Reflections on Gender and Science[18] by Evelyn Fox Keller

Coalition/Opposition Breakdown: 60/40

Evelyn Fox Keller's book leans towards the coalition's viewpoint as it explores the gendered nature of science and its historical development. The book delves into how science evolved into a male-dominated field, aligning with the coalition's emphasis on historical underrepresentation. However, Keller's nuanced discussion, including the rejection of the notion of a "female way of doing science," shows an appreciation for merit-based principles in science, aligning slightly with the opposition's viewpoint.

Dorothy Hodgkin[19] by Georgina Ferry

Coalition/Opposition Breakdown: 80/20

This biography of Dorothy Hodgkin heavily supports the coalition's viewpoint by highlighting the remarkable achievements of a woman scientist who excelled in her field despite the challenges of her time. Hodgkin's story of balancing her scientific career and family life aligns with the coalition's emphasis on recognizing and

---

[18] https://amzn.to/47Lk2Fc
[19] https://amzn.to/487Ya6y

celebrating women's contributions in STEM. The lesser alignment with the opposition's viewpoint comes from Hodgkin's success within the existing system of her time, suggesting some level of functionality in merit-based structures.

Chapter 5: Women's Rights in the 20th Century

"The most courageous act is still to think for yourself. Aloud" - Coco Chanel

Progress and Setbacks: Analyze the progress made in women's rights during the 20th century, including the feminist movements, and the backlash or setbacks experienced.

The heart of the debate on women's rights in the 20th century is centered around the role of women in society, which encapsulates both the progress and setbacks of the feminist movement. This aspect is highly polarizing because it challenges deep-rooted societal norms and cultural expectations about gender roles.

The 20th century saw remarkable progress in women's rights, most notably in areas like voting rights, access to education, and employment opportunities. The feminist movements played a pivotal role, advocating for equality and challenging the traditional view that women's primary role was in the home. This push for change led to significant legal and social reforms, granting women more control over their lives and bodies, particularly in the latter half of the century.

However, this progress did not come without resistance. The core of the contention lies in the differing views on the extent and nature of women's roles. On one hand, feminists argued for complete equality, asserting that women should have the same opportunities as men in every aspect of society. They fought against discriminatory practices and sought to dismantle the patriarchal structures that limited women's potential.

On the other side, conservative and traditional viewpoints held that certain roles and responsibilities were inherently suited to men or women. This perspective often stemmed from cultural, religious, or historical beliefs about gender. Critics of the feminist movement argued that efforts to radically alter women's roles could undermine family structures and societal stability.

This clash of viewpoints led to intense debates and sometimes backlash against feminist achievements. For example, the push for workplace equality was met with concerns about the impact on family life, particularly the upbringing of children. Similarly, the sexual revolution and reproductive rights movements of the late 20th century were contentious, with opposition often grounded in moral or religious arguments.

The debate over women's roles remains contentious because it touches on deeply personal and societal values. It's not just a debate about laws or policies, but about how we define and value different roles within our society. This ongoing discussion reflects the evolving nature of our understanding of gender equality and the continuous struggle to balance individual rights with cultural and societal norms.

Coalition Speech (Progressive Viewpoint)

In support of the implementation of policies and social reforms to ensure complete gender equality in all aspects of society

Ladies and gentlemen, esteemed members of this house, today we stand at a pivotal moment in our collective journey towards equality and justice. Our motion, "This house supports the implementation of policies and social reforms to ensure complete gender equality in all aspects of society," is not just a call for action; it is a testament to our unwavering commitment to the rights and dignity of every individual.

Let us begin by journeying back through history, to the early 20th century when women first raised their voices demanding the right to vote. This watershed moment was not just about ballots; it was about recognizing women as equal citizens in the very fabric of our society. Fast forward to the present, and we see women making strides in education and professional fields, breaking barriers that once seemed insurmountable. However, this journey is far from complete. The persisting wage gaps, the underrepresentation in leadership roles, and the ongoing struggles for reproductive rights and healthcare access underscore the critical need for our motion.

Now, consider the broader tapestry of our society. Imagine a world where gender equality is not just an ideal, but a reality. Economically, the inclusion of women in the workforce is not merely a matter of fairness; it is a catalyst for growth and prosperity. Diverse leadership in companies is not just about representation; it's about enhancing decision-making and driving better outcomes. The societal benefits of gender equality extend far beyond the economic sphere. In societies where gender equality flourishes, we witness lower rates of domestic violence and better health outcomes. It's a world where every individual, regardless of gender, can contribute to and benefit from a healthier, more prosperous, and more equitable society.

But at the heart of our motion lies something even more fundamental – the ethical imperative of equality. Gender equality is not a privilege; it is a fundamental human right, enshrined in international treaties and declarations. It's about recognizing the inherent dignity and worth of every individual. Our motion is not just about policies and reforms; it's about rectifying the historical injustices that have long silenced and marginalized women. It's about taking a stand against discrimination and affirming our commitment to a world where everyone, regardless of gender, has the opportunity to live a life of dignity, respect, and fulfillment.

Ladies and gentlemen, as we stand here today, let us remember that this motion is more than just words on a paper. It is a promise – a promise to future generations that we will not rest until we have built a world where gender equality is not just an aspiration, but a reality. It's a commitment to tear down the barriers of discrimination and build bridges of understanding and respect. This is our time to shape a future where equality is the norm, not the exception.

In conclusion, this house must support the motion, not just for the sake of women, but for the sake of humanity. For in the words of the great poet Maya Angelou, "Each time a woman stands up for herself, she stands up for all women." Today, let us stand up for gender equality, for justice, for progress. Let us stand up for a world where every voice is heard, and every dream is valued. Thank you.

Opposition Speech (Conservative Viewpoint)

Opposed to the radical restructuring of societal norms and maintains the importance of traditional gender roles in maintaining societal stability and cultural values

Ladies and gentlemen, esteemed members of this house, today we gather to discuss a motion that stands at the crossroads of tradition and change. As we deliberate, let us remember that our roots, our traditions, and our cultural values are the bedrock of our society. The opposition's stance is clear: we oppose the radical restructuring of societal norms and firmly believe in the importance of traditional gender roles in maintaining societal stability and upholding our cherished cultural values.

Firstly, let us consider the historical continuity of our social structures. For centuries, traditional gender roles have provided a framework for societal stability and harmony. This structure is not a relic of the past; rather, it is a testament to a tried and tested system that has ensured the smooth functioning of societies across the globe. Abrupt changes to these roles can lead to confusion and conflict, threatening the very fabric of our cultural identity. Moreover, the stability of the family unit, integral to our social structure, is underpinned by these traditional roles. Evidence has consistently shown that children raised in stable, two-parent homes excel socially and educationally, highlighting the importance of preserving these roles for the well-being of future generations.

Moving to our cultural and moral values, we must acknowledge that many cultures have deep-rooted traditions regarding gender roles. These traditions form a crucial part of our collective identity. To disregard them is to disregard our heritage. Furthermore, these roles often align with moral and ethical standards that have guided human societies for centuries. A sudden departure from these roles not only undermines our cultural legacy but also raises profound ethical concerns.

Lastly, we must address the practicality and natural differences between genders. Biological and psychological differences are not social constructs; they are realities. Recognizing and respecting these differences is not regressive; it is a rational acknowledgment of nature. In certain sectors, such as defense or heavy industry, these differences might mean that roles are more effectively filled by one gender over the other. This recognition leads to more efficient functioning in various aspects of our society and economy.

In conclusion, while we acknowledge the strides made in women's rights, we must also recognize the value and importance of our traditions and cultural norms. Our motion is not a stand against progress; it is a stand for balance, for respect towards our heritage, and for the practical realities of our nature. As we move forward, let us not forget the foundations upon which our societies are built. I urge this house to consider the implications of radical changes and to uphold the values that have stood the test of time. Thank you.

Challenging questions

10 questions from the coalition to the opposition:

1. How do you reconcile the historical exclusion and marginalization of women in traditional gender roles with the modern principles of equality and human rights?
2. What evidence can you provide to support the claim that traditional gender roles, rather than individual choice and

merit, lead to better outcomes in family and societal stability?

3. In what ways do you believe that biological differences between genders should dictate social, professional, and personal opportunities in the 21st century?

4. How does the opposition's viewpoint address the economic and social benefits that have been proven to arise from greater gender equality in the workforce and leadership positions?

5. Can you elaborate on how the preservation of traditional gender roles aligns with the evolving nature of global cultures, where gender norms are continuously shifting?

6. How would you respond to the argument that traditional gender roles often perpetuate harmful stereotypes and limit the potential of both men and women?

7. In societies where traditional gender roles have been relaxed or redefined, what negative impacts, if any, have been definitively observed that can be directly attributed to this change?

8. How do you propose to address the aspirations and rights of individuals who feel constrained or misrepresented by traditional gender roles?

9. What is your response to the argument that insistence on traditional gender roles in a rapidly evolving world might hinder a country's global competitiveness and innovation?

10. How would you suggest dealing with the discrepancy between the preservation of traditional gender roles and the increasing demand for equal treatment and opportunities for women in many societies?

10 questions from the opposition to the coalition:

1. How do you propose to balance the pursuit of gender equality with respect for cultural traditions and values that place importance on traditional gender roles?

2. What measures would you suggest to ensure that the push for gender equality does not inadvertently lead to reverse discrimination or the overlooking of merit in sectors like employment and education?

3. In your view, how can we address the biological and physiological differences between genders in certain professions without compromising on the principle of equality?

4. Can you provide empirical evidence that demonstrates a direct causal relationship between gender equality policies and the claimed economic and societal benefits?

5. How does the coalition's viewpoint account for the potential negative impacts on family stability and child development when both parents are heavily engaged in the workforce due to policies promoting complete gender equality?

6. How would you address concerns that policies aimed at enforcing gender equality might lead to governmental overreach into private business practices and individual choices?

7. In what ways can the coalition ensure that the drive for gender equality does not diminish the value and choice of those who prefer traditional gender roles, either by personal choice or cultural influence?

8. Can you provide historical examples where the rapid implementation of gender equality policies has led to sustainable, long-term societal benefits without significant cultural backlash?

9. How does the coalition plan to reconcile differences within the feminist movement itself, where views on gender roles and equality measures often vary significantly?

10. How will the coalition address the complexity of gender issues in diverse societies, where cultural, religious, and socio-economic factors significantly influence perceptions and realities of gender equality?

Potential solutions to reconcile the two parties

In navigating the complex terrain of women's rights and the interplay between progress and tradition, it becomes clear that a path of mutual understanding and compromise is not only possible but essential. At the heart of this journey lies the shared goal of fostering a society that honors both equality and respect for diverse perspectives.

The first step in this journey could be the **implementation of flexible policies** that accommodate both traditional and modern roles. This approach respects individual choice, allowing people to opt for traditional roles or progressive paths without facing societal judgment or disadvantage.

Education plays a pivotal role in this compromise. By **incorporating gender studies into educational curricula**, we can foster an understanding of both the historical context of gender roles and the importance of gender equality. This balanced educational approach can cultivate respect for diverse viewpoints.

At the workplace, a pragmatic solution lies in developing policies that recognize both merit and the need for equal opportunities. For instance, **implementing transparent hiring practices** that emphasize qualifications, while also encouraging diversity, can be a balanced approach. Moreover, companies could offer **flexible work arrangements** such as telecommuting or flexible hours, which can be particularly beneficial for parents, irrespective of gender.

In terms of addressing societal roles and expectations, public campaigns and community programs can play a significant role. **Public awareness campaigns** that highlight the value of both traditional and non-traditional roles can foster a culture of respect and choice. Simultaneously, **community support programs** can provide resources and support for those who choose non-traditional paths, such as stay-at-home fathers or women in leadership roles.

On the more contentious issue of reproductive rights and healthcare, a balanced approach could involve **ensuring access to healthcare and reproductive services** while also respecting the diverse ethical and religious beliefs in society. This could involve providing comprehensive sex education and access to contraception, reducing the need for more divisive measures.

Policies that support family stability, such as **parental leave and childcare support**, can also bridge the gap. These policies benefit all families, whether they adhere to traditional roles or not, by easing the burden of childcare and supporting parents in the workforce.

In the political arena, encouraging diverse representation in government can ensure that all viewpoints are considered in policymaking. This could involve **implementing measures to encourage women's participation in politics**, while also respecting the perspectives of those with more traditional views.

Economic policies can also play a role in finding middle ground. For example, **tax incentives for companies that demonstrate gender parity** in leadership roles can encourage equality without mandating it, offering a compromise between regulatory imposition and laissez-faire approaches.

Lastly, **regular forums for dialogue between different groups** can ensure ongoing communication and understanding. These forums can serve as platforms for discussing new policies, sharing concerns, and adjusting approaches as society evolves.

By weaving together these various strands of policy, education, workplace practices, societal support, and dialogue, we can create a tapestry that respects both the desire for progress and the importance of tradition. This balanced approach allows for a society that is both forward-looking and respectful of its roots, where choices are respected, and diversity is seen as a strength.

Identifying Viewpoints

Identify the Progressive Viewpoint:

What: The progressive viewpoint in the debate on women's rights in the 20th century is centered on the advocacy for complete equality between genders in all aspects of society. This includes equal opportunities in education, employment, political representation, and reproductive rights.

Why: This aspect is considered progressive because it emphasizes change and challenges the traditional societal roles assigned to women. It aligns with progressive ideologies through its focus on social reform and the modern interpretation of gender roles. The progressive viewpoint advocates for dismantling patriarchal structures and discriminatory practices, seeking to establish a society where gender does not dictate one's opportunities or rights. This viewpoint is underpinned by a belief in equality, personal autonomy, and the evolving nature of societal norms.

Identify the Conservative Viewpoint:

What: The conservative viewpoint in this debate is the emphasis on traditional gender roles, advocating for the preservation of established norms regarding the different roles and responsibilities of men and women in society.

Why: This aspect is considered conservative as it focuses on maintaining the status quo and upholding historical and cultural beliefs about gender. It often draws on religious, moral, or traditional arguments to support the idea that certain roles are inherently suited to men or women. This viewpoint values the preservation of traditional family structures and often perceives radical changes to women's roles as potentially destabilizing to societal stability. The conservative perspective is characterized by a cautious approach to social change, emphasizing the importance of continuity and the preservation of established norms and values.

Political Analysis

Progressive/Liberal (Left) Viewpoints:

In support of complete gender equality (progressive aspect): A large segment of the left, let's hypothetically estimate around 70%, views gender equality as a fundamental goal. This group strongly supports equal rights and opportunities for women in all areas, including workplace, politics, education, and reproductive rights. They advocate for policies and reforms that dismantle gender-based discrimination and promote gender neutrality in all aspects of society.

In support of some traditional gender roles (conservative aspect): A smaller portion of the left, hypothetically around 30%, might support certain aspects of traditional gender roles. This group might believe in the importance of some gender-specific roles, particularly in the context of family and child-rearing, or may have concerns about the pace of societal changes related to gender. They often focus on balancing progress with the preservation of some traditional values.

Conservative/Republican (Right) Viewpoints:

In support of some aspects of gender equality (progressive aspect): A portion of the conservative side, let's say about 40%, might support certain aspects of gender equality. This group recognizes the need for equal rights in specific areas like education and employment but might differ on issues like reproductive rights or the extent of gender neutrality in societal roles. They tend to support gradual, incremental changes rather than radical reforms.

In support of traditional gender roles (conservative aspect): The majority of the conservative viewpoint, estimated at 60%, likely emphasizes the importance of traditional gender roles. This group values historical and cultural norms regarding gender, often citing religious, moral, or traditional justifications for maintaining distinct roles for men and women, particularly in family settings. They often view changes to these roles as potentially disruptive to societal stability.

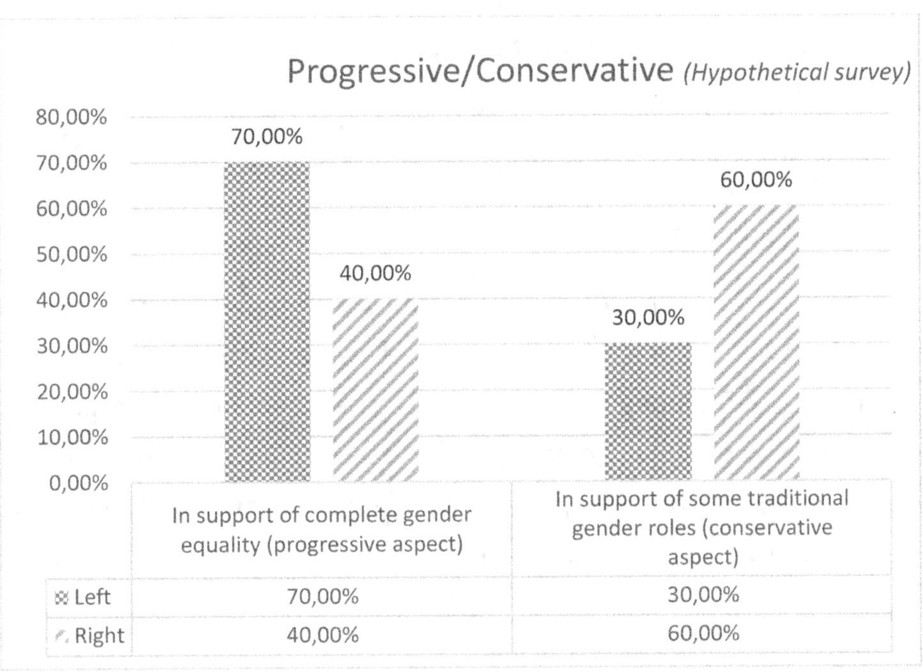

	In support of complete gender equality (progressive aspect)	In support of some traditional gender roles (conservative aspect)
Left	70,00%	30,00%
Right	40,00%	60,00%

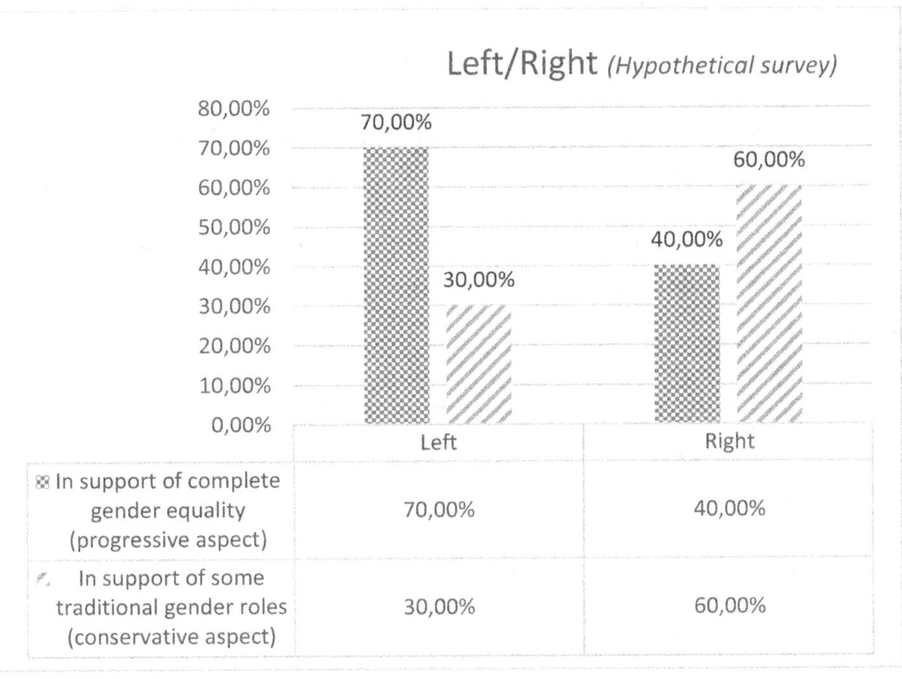

	Left	Right
In support of complete gender equality (progressive aspect)	70,00%	40,00%
In support of some traditional gender roles (conservative aspect)	30,00%	60,00%

Recommended Resources

Hood Feminism[20] by Mikki Kendall

Coalition/Opposition Breakdown: 70/30

Kendall's critique of the modern feminist movement for its failure to address the needs of all women leans towards the coalition's perspective of advocating for broader and more inclusive gender equality. However, its critique of the existing feminist movement also resonates with the opposition's concerns about the direction of current gender equality movements.

All In[21] by Billie Jean King, Johnette Howard, and Maryanne Vollers

Coalition/Opposition Breakdown: 80/20

This book's focus on Billie Jean King's activism and commitment to fairness and social justice strongly aligns with the coalition's push for gender equality. It slightly accommodates the opposition in recognizing the struggles within the journey of achieving these goals.

---

[20] https://amzn.to/41dOe9F
[21] https://amzn.to/47MZIDe

My Life on the Road[22] by Gloria Steinem

Coalition/Opposition Breakdown: 90/10

Steinem's narrative as a feminist activist aligns predominantly with the coalition's perspective, advocating for gender equality and reform. The slight alignment with the opposition comes from acknowledging the complexities and challenges faced in the journey of activism.

Know My Name[23] by Chanel Miller

Coalition/Opposition Breakdown: 95/5

Miller's account, which highlights the issues of sexual assault and the importance of voice and identity, strongly supports the coalition's stance on women's rights and empowerment. The minimal alignment with the opposition is in acknowledging the societal and legal challenges in addressing these issues.

The Handmaid's Tale[24] by Margaret Atwood

Coalition/Opposition Breakdown: 100/0

Atwood's dystopian novel, portraying the extreme loss of women's rights, aligns entirely with the coalition's perspective by highlighting

---

[22] https://amzn.to/46HWqQB
[23] https://amzn.to/3RaZpv8
[24] https://amzn.to/41aEP2q

the dangers of completely eroding women's rights and the importance of fighting against such futures.

Unwell Women[25] by Elinor Cleghorn

Coalition/Opposition Breakdown: 90/10

The exploration of how medicine has historically failed women aligns strongly with the coalition's advocacy for comprehensive gender equality, particularly in healthcare. The slight accommodation of the opposition's viewpoint is in recognizing the historical context of these failures.

Entitled[26] by Kate Manne

Coalition/Opposition Breakdown: 85/15

Manne's exploration of gender, power, and entitlement aligns largely with the coalition's viewpoint on addressing gender-based inequalities and biases. The partial alignment with the opposition comes from a critical examination of existing power structures and societal norms.

---

[25] https://amzn.to/3NiQdDM
[26] https://amzn.to/3uP9zKk

<u>*Women, Race & Class*</u>[27] by Angela Y. Davis

Coalition/Opposition Breakdown: 75/25

Davis's examination of the intersectionality of race, class, and gender in feminism largely supports the coalition's perspective on broadening the scope of gender equality movements. However, it also resonates with the opposition in terms of respecting the complexities and diverse experiences within the feminist movement.

<u>*The Great Stewardess Rebellion*</u>[28] by Nell McShane Wulfhart

Coalition/Opposition Breakdown: 80/20

The story of stewardesses standing up against corporations aligns with the coalition's viewpoint of advocating for women's rights in the workplace, while also acknowledging the opposition's perspective on the practical challenges and negotiations involved in such movements.

<u>*She Said*</u>[29] by Jodi Kantor and Megan Twohey

Coalition/Opposition Breakdown: 90/10

The narrative of breaking the Harvey Weinstein scandal and its impact on the #MeToo movement strongly aligns with the coalition's emphasis on addressing and challenging systemic

---

[27] https://amzn.to/3R8xJad
[28] https://amzn.to/47Lsog2
[29] https://amzn.to/3R8Xd7j

gender-based abuses and inequalities. The slight alignment with the opposition comes from recognizing the societal and institutional challenges in these endeavors.

Chapter 6: The Role of Women in War and Peace

"I do not believe in using women in combat, because females are too fierce." - Margaret Mead

Discuss the roles women have played in war (as combatants, spies, nurses) and peace movements across different cultures and eras, and how these roles have shaped societal views on women.

The most polarizing aspect of the role of women in war and peace lies in the ongoing debate about their participation in direct combat roles. Historically, women's roles in warfare were often limited to support functions such as nursing, intelligence gathering, and maintaining the home front. However, as societies have evolved, women have increasingly taken on more direct roles in military operations, including as combatants. This shift has sparked intense debate, stirring the traditional views on gender roles and the capabilities of women in high-risk, physically demanding situations.

On one side of the debate, proponents argue for gender equality in all spheres, including the military. They contend that women possess the same abilities as men to contribute effectively in combat roles and that their inclusion can bring diverse perspectives and skills to military operations. This viewpoint often emphasizes the examples of historical and contemporary female warriors who have demonstrated bravery and skill on par with their male counterparts.

In contrast, opponents of women in combat roles often cite physical differences, the potential impact on unit cohesion, and concerns about the treatment of female prisoners of war. They argue that the inclusion of women in front-line combat might compromise military effectiveness due to perceived physical limitations and the challenges of integrating women into traditionally male-dominated military units.

This debate is so contentious because it touches on deeply ingrained societal norms and beliefs about gender. It challenges long-standing views of masculinity and femininity, especially in the context of war, which has traditionally been seen as the ultimate test of masculinity. The discussion is not just about physical capabilities or military tactics; it's deeply intertwined with cultural, psychological, and social dimensions of gender identity.

The ongoing debate reflects broader societal tensions regarding gender equality and roles. It exemplifies the complexities of integrating women into roles historically dominated by men, not just in the military, but across various sectors of society. As such, the conversation continues to evolve, mirroring the changing landscape of gender dynamics in the modern world.

Coalition Speech (Progressive Viewpoint)

In support of the full integration of women in combat roles within the military

Ladies and gentlemen, esteemed members of this house, we stand at a pivotal crossroads in history. Today, we gather not just to debate a motion, but to affirm a fundamental truth: the full integration of women in combat roles within the military is not only necessary, but imperative for our progress as a society.

Let us begin by addressing the heart of this matter - gender equality and military effectiveness. History is replete with tales of women who have not only participated in combat but have excelled. From the ancient warrior queens to the valiant women soldiers of today, women have proven time and again their capability on the battlefield. Consider the story of the Night Witches, an all-female Soviet air force unit in World War II. They struck fear into the hearts of their enemies, not just because of their gender, but because of their unyielding bravery and skill. This is not just about granting rights; it's about recognizing abilities that have been evident throughout history.

But let's delve deeper. Our argument is not just rooted in the past, but in the potential for a more effective and innovative future. Diversity in the military, including gender diversity, brings a wealth of perspectives that are invaluable in complex, global conflicts. It's about harnessing the full spectrum of human talent and insight for better problem-solving and strategy.

Now, let's turn our gaze to the broader societal impact. The integration of women into combat roles shatters archaic stereotypes. It sends a powerful message to our daughters and sons about the limitless potential of an individual, irrespective of gender. When women serve alongside men in the heat of battle, it redefines bravery and strength in our cultural psyche. We are not just talking about reforming an institution; we're talking about transforming societal norms.

Moreover, let's not overlook the unique contributions women can make in peacebuilding. Studies have shown that peace agreements involving women are more durable. When women, who often bear the brunt of war's horrors, are involved in peace negotiations, their perspectives create more comprehensive and lasting peace solutions.

But let's also address the here and now - the modern military needs. Warfare today is not just about brute strength; it's about intelligence, technology, and adaptability. The physical differences between genders pale in comparison to the need for mental agility and technological prowess. The military needs the best, and the best cannot be defined by gender.

Finally, consider the practical aspect. Expanding the talent pool to include women in combat roles addresses critical personnel shortages in the military. It's not just a matter of principle, but of practicality.

So, I urge this house to look forward, not backward. To see the integration of women in combat roles not as a challenge to overcome, but an opportunity to embrace. Let us not limit our potential based on antiquated notions of gender. Let us, instead, unleash it for a stronger, more effective, and equitable future.

This house must support the full integration of women in combat roles within the military, for in doing so, we are not just changing an institution; we are changing the very fabric of society for the better. Thank you.

Opposition Speech (Conservative Viewpoint)

Opposed to the integration of women in direct combat roles, maintaining traditional gender roles within the military

Ladies and gentlemen of this esteemed house, today we stand not only to voice an opposition but to uphold a time-honored tradition, one rooted in practical wisdom and historical precedent. Our motion, "This house opposes the integration of women in direct combat roles, maintaining traditional gender roles within the military," is not a stance against progress, but a call for prudence and respect for the complexities of warfare.

Let us first examine the crux of military effectiveness: physical capability and unit cohesion. Studies and history show us that the rigorous physical demands of combat often exceed the average physical capabilities of women. This is not a statement on women's overall abilities but an acknowledgment of inherent physical differences that can impact combat performance and, by extension, mission success. We remember instances in history where physical limitations have been a decisive factor in the outcome of military engagements.

Moving to unit cohesion, a cornerstone of military success, we find that the integration of women into combat roles presents significant challenges. Mixed-gender units in high-stress combat situations face unique dynamics that can affect morale and effectiveness. Historical examples abound where integration, albeit well-intentioned, has inadvertently led to decreased unit cohesion.

Turning to the historical and cultural context, we must recognize the weight of tradition. Military institutions worldwide have long-established gender roles deeply intertwined with the cultural fabric of societies. To upend these roles is not merely a change in policy; it is a disruption of a cultural ethos that has defined military structures for centuries. When we consider altering such fundamental aspects, we must ponder the societal repercussions and the message it sends about gender roles.

Moreover, the practical and logistical concerns of integrating women into combat roles cannot be understated. The requirements for separate facilities, equipment adaptations, and training regimes present significant logistical hurdles. These challenges extend beyond mere inconvenience; they necessitate a complete overhaul of established military systems, incurring substantial costs and resource allocation.

Finally, we must address a grave concern: the safety of women in combat, particularly as prisoners of war. Historical accounts reveal the harrowing experiences of female combatants when captured. The risk of sexual violence and harsh treatment is a grim reality that cannot be ignored in this debate.

In conclusion, while the motion presented by the coalition is laudable in its pursuit of equality, it overlooks critical factors that underpin military effectiveness, tradition, and practicality. Our stance is one of realism, rooted in an understanding of the complex nature of warfare and the sanctity of established military traditions. We must tread this path with caution, respecting the nuances and the high stakes involved. Therefore, this house must oppose the integration of women in direct combat roles, not as a barrier to progress, but as a bastion of practical wisdom and historical insight. Thank you.

Challenging questions

10 questions from the coalition to the opposition:

1. How do you reconcile the exclusion of women from combat roles with the principle of equal opportunity, especially given the examples of women successfully serving in these roles in various countries?
2. In light of modern warfare's increasing reliance on technology and strategy over brute physical strength, how do you justify the continued emphasis on physical differences as a barrier to women's participation in combat?
3. Can you provide empirical evidence demonstrating that mixed-gender military units have significantly lower cohesion or effectiveness compared to single-gender units?
4. How do you address the argument that excluding women from combat roles perpetuates outdated stereotypes about gender capabilities, potentially hindering broader societal progress towards gender equality?
5. Considering the successful integration of women into the armed forces of countries like Israel and Canada, what specific factors make their experiences inapplicable or irrelevant to other nations?
6. How does maintaining traditional gender roles in the military align with the evolving societal views on gender

equality and the changing nature of family and professional roles?

7. What measures could be implemented to mitigate your concerns about physical differences and unit cohesion, rather than outright banning women from combat roles?

8. How do you respond to studies showing that the inclusion of women in peace processes leads to more sustainable and comprehensive peace agreements?

9. Given the historical examples of women serving effectively in combat roles, such as during World War II, how do you justify the claim that women inherently lack the capabilities for such roles?

10. If the primary concern is the safety and well-being of women in combat, why not advocate for improved protections and support systems rather than excluding them from these roles altogether?

10 questions from the opposition to the coalition:

1. How do you propose to address the physiological differences between men and women, especially in regards to the physical demands of certain combat roles?

2. What measures would you implement to ensure that the integration of women into combat roles does not negatively impact unit cohesion and military effectiveness?

3. How would you respond to concerns about the potential increase in sexual harassment and assault cases with the integration of women into close-quarter combat environments?

4. Can you provide concrete evidence showing that mixed-gender combat units perform as effectively as single-gender units in high-intensity combat situations?

5. In light of the historical treatment of female prisoners of war, what steps would you take to ensure the safety and humane treatment of women captured in combat?

6. How would you manage the additional logistical challenges and costs associated with integrating women into combat roles, such as the need for separate living quarters and specialized medical care?

7. How do you address the argument that the push for gender equality in the military might come at the expense of operational effectiveness and readiness?

8. Given the varying physical standards for men and women in most militaries, how would you ensure fairness and maintain rigorous standards in physical training and testing for combat roles?

9. Can you provide examples of how the integration of women into combat roles has directly contributed to better outcomes in military operations or conflicts?

10. How do you plan to reconcile the cultural and psychological challenges faced by both men and women when adapting to mixed-gender combat units, especially in societies with strong traditional views on gender roles?

Potential solutions to reconcile the two parties

In the quest to bridge the gap between the coalition's push for the full integration of women in combat roles and the opposition's concerns for maintaining traditional gender roles in the military, we find ourselves navigating a complex landscape. The key to finding common ground lies in understanding and addressing the concerns of both sides through thoughtful compromises and solutions.

We begin with the **implementation of gender-neutral physical standards**. This approach respects the need for operational effectiveness, ensuring that all combatants, regardless of gender, meet the same rigorous criteria. Such standards would address the opposition's concerns about physical capabilities while upholding the coalition's desire for equality.

Acknowledging the challenges of integration, a solution could be the **development of mixed-gender units with specialized roles**. These units could capitalize on the diverse strengths of both men and women, ensuring that physical differences are not a hindrance but rather a strategic advantage. This approach could serve as a pilot program, allowing for assessment and adjustments, ensuring that both operational effectiveness and integration are achieved.

To address concerns about unit cohesion, the military could invest in **comprehensive training programs focusing on teamwork and mutual respect**. These programs would foster a culture of inclusivity and understanding, addressing the opposition's concerns about unit dynamics while furthering the coalition's goal of integration.

The issue of safety, particularly for women in combat roles, is paramount. Here, the establishment of **strict protocols and support systems to address sexual harassment and assault** is crucial. This ensures a safe working environment for everyone, addressing a core concern of the opposition while aligning with the coalition's goals of equal opportunity.

Recognizing the historical treatment of female prisoners of war, the military could develop **specialized training for women in evasion and survival techniques**, equipping them with the skills to handle such scenarios. This would alleviate some of the opposition's concerns about women's safety in combat roles.

To mitigate the logistical challenges of integration, the military could explore **modular living and facility solutions**. These would offer flexibility, catering to the needs of mixed-gender units without significant disruptions or additional costs.

In terms of operational readiness, a balanced approach could involve **assigning women to combat roles based on strategic needs and individual capabilities**. This method respects the coalition's desire for integration while addressing the opposition's concerns about effectiveness.

Another area of compromise could be the **establishment of a task force to monitor and evaluate the integration process**. This task force, comprised of members from both sides of the debate, would ensure that the concerns of both parties are continually addressed and that the integration process is effective and respectful of all service members.

To further ease the transition, the military could offer **counseling services and support groups for both men and women**. These services would help service members adapt to the new dynamics of mixed-gender units, aligning with both sides' interest in maintaining a strong and cohesive military force.

Lastly, the integration process could be approached as a **phased implementation**, starting with specific branches or units where the integration of women could be more easily managed. This gradual approach allows for learning and adjustments, ensuring a smoother transition to full integration.

Through these solutions, we weave a narrative of compromise and mutual respect, addressing the key concerns of both the coalition and the opposition. It's a journey of finding a middle ground where operational effectiveness, equality, and the well-being of all service members are harmoniously balanced.

Identifying Viewpoints

Identify the Progressive Viewpoint:

What: The advocacy for women's participation in direct combat roles in the military.

Why: This aspect is considered progressive as it aligns with ideologies that focus on change, social reform, and equality. The progressive viewpoint emphasizes breaking traditional gender norms and roles, advocating for equal opportunities for women in all areas, including those historically dominated by men. It is rooted in the belief that women and men are equally capable and should be afforded the same rights and opportunities, including serving in combat roles in the military. This perspective often highlights the evolution of societal roles and challenges traditional conceptions of femininity and masculinity, reflecting a modern interpretation of gender equality.

Identify the Conservative Viewpoint:

What: The opposition to women serving in direct combat roles in the military.

Why: This viewpoint is considered conservative as it aligns with the preservation of traditional roles and norms, particularly regarding gender roles in a historical context. The conservative perspective often emphasizes the differences between men and women, citing physical, psychological, and social reasons for maintaining traditional gender roles in the military. This viewpoint tends to prioritize the preservation of established norms and the perceived effectiveness of the military structure as it has historically functioned. It reflects a cautious approach to changing long-standing institutions and roles, valuing historical precedent and the perceived stability it provides.

Political Analysis

Progressive/Liberal (Left) Viewpoints:

In support of women in combat roles (progressive aspect): A significant portion of the left likely views the inclusion of women in combat roles positively. This group advocates for gender equality and sees this as a step towards breaking traditional gender barriers. They might argue that women are just as capable as men in these roles and that their inclusion is a progressive move towards a more inclusive military. Estimated representation: 70%.

In support of traditional gender roles in military (conservative aspect): A smaller segment within the left might support more traditional views, possibly due to concerns about physical capabilities, the impact on unit cohesion, or other logistical challenges in integrating women into combat roles. This group, while generally supportive of gender equality, might favor a more cautious approach to the integration of women in direct combat. Estimated representation: 30%.

Conservative/Republican (Right) Viewpoints:

In support of women in combat roles (progressive aspect): Within the conservative camp, there may be a minority who support the idea of women in combat roles. This group might view it as an extension of individual rights and capabilities, emphasizing that capable individuals, regardless of gender, should have the opportunity to serve in any military capacity. Estimated representation: 25%.

In support of traditional gender roles in military (conservative aspect): The majority on the right might favor maintaining traditional gender roles in the military. This viewpoint often stems from concerns over physical differences between genders, potential impacts on unit dynamics, and the historical precedent of men in combat roles. This group likely views the existing structure as effective and sees significant changes as potentially disruptive. Estimated representation: 75%.

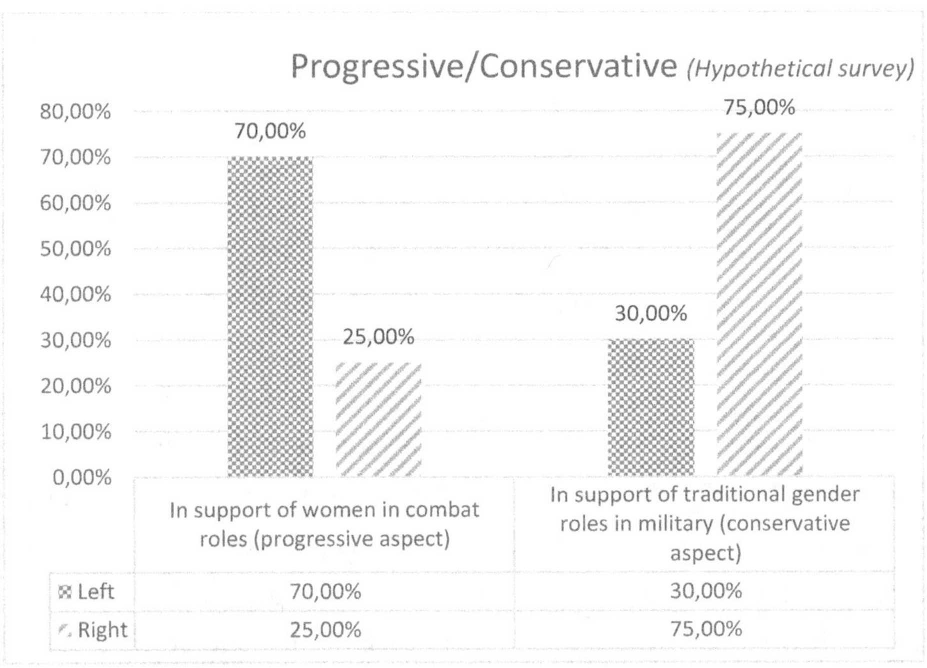

	In support of women in combat roles (progressive aspect)	In support of traditional gender roles in military (conservative aspect)
Left	70,00%	30,00%
Right	25,00%	75,00%

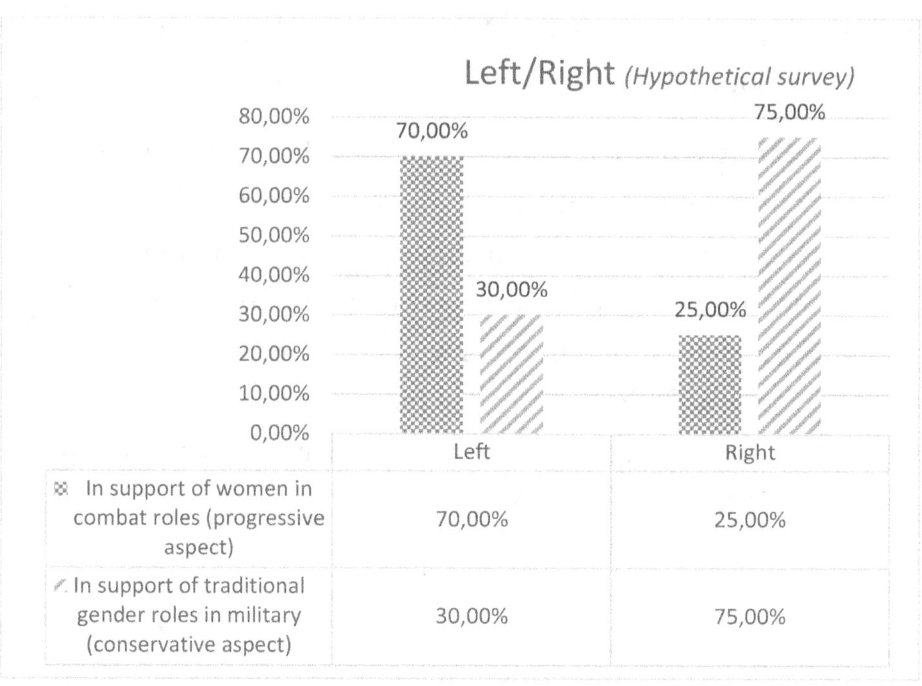

	Left	Right
⊠ In support of women in combat roles (progressive aspect)	70,00%	25,00%
⬚ In support of traditional gender roles in military (conservative aspect)	30,00%	75,00%

Recommended Resources

The Selected Letters of Martha Gellhorn[30] by Caroline Moorehead

Coalition/Opposition Breakdown: 60/40

This book slightly leans towards the coalition's viewpoint, as it showcases Martha Gellhorn's experiences and observations as a war correspondent and writer. Gellhorn's letters provide insight into her strong, independent character and her role in war, which aligns with the coalition's emphasis on women's capabilities and contributions in conflict situations. However, the book also touches on the

---

[30] https://amzn.to/3GwnG9R

challenges and societal expectations she faced, reflecting some concerns of the opposition.

Emma's War[31] by Deborah Scroggins

Coalition/Opposition Breakdown: 70/30

"Emma's War" predominantly aligns with the coalition's viewpoint by depicting the life of Emma McCune, a British aid worker in Sudan, who broke traditional gender roles. Her marriage to a rebel warlord and her involvement in complex political scenarios highlight women's active participation in conflict zones, supporting the coalition's stance. However, the disastrous consequences of her actions and the exploration of the moral dilemmas surrounding humanitarian aid also resonate with some of the opposition's concerns about the complexities and risks involved in women's direct engagement in war zones.

Mighty Be Our Powers[32] by Leymah Gwobee

Coalition/Opposition Breakdown: 80/20

This book strongly aligns with the coalition's viewpoint. It tells the story of Leymah Gwobee, who led a peace movement in Liberia, demonstrating the powerful role women can play in resolving conflicts and building peace. Gbowee's journey from a young mother in a war-torn country to an international leader symbolizes

---

[31] https://amzn.to/488tX7q
[32] https://amzn.to/47OUozw

the coalition's argument about women's capabilities in war and peace. The emphasis on sisterhood and collective action of women also underlines the coalition's stance on gender equality. However, it slightly touches upon the traditional struggles and challenges faced by women in conflict, which aligns with some of the opposition's viewpoints.

The Girls Come Marching Home[33] by Kirsten Holmstedt

Coalition/Opposition Breakdown: 75/25

This book aligns more with the coalition's viewpoint by sharing deeply personal accounts of American women soldiers returning from the Iraq War. It highlights the courage, resilience, and struggles of women in combat and post-combat scenarios, which aligns with the coalition's arguments about women's roles in direct combat and the broader impacts on their lives. However, the book also acknowledges the psychological and physical wounds these women warriors face, which resonates with some of the opposition's concerns about the well-being and safety of women in combat roles.

---

[33] https://amzn.to/3uLFdse

Chapter 7: Women in Art and Literature

Debate the representation and contributions of women in art and literature, examining how female artists and writers have been historically perceived and the evolution of female characters in literature.

The heart of the debate surrounding women in art and literature centers on the recognition and representation of female artists and characters. Historically, the arts and literary fields were predominantly male-dominated, with women often marginalized or their contributions minimized. This led to a skewed representation of women, both as creators and as subjects in art and literature. The core of the contention lies in how female artists and writers have been perceived and the evolution of female characters in literature, reflecting broader societal attitudes towards women.

One side of the debate argues that historical underrepresentation and stereotyping of women in these fields have led to a significant gap in the cultural and literary canon. Advocates for this viewpoint stress the need to re-evaluate and elevate the work of female artists and writers, both past and present, to correct these imbalances. They contend that the traditional narrative has often ignored or undervalued the contributions of women, leading to a limited and sometimes distorted view of women's roles and abilities.

On the other side, some argue that the current emphasis on gender can overshadow artistic merit, advocating for a more 'neutral' approach where art and literature are judged irrespective of the creator's gender. They fear that an overcorrection could lead to a form of reverse discrimination, where the focus shifts from quality to identity.

The polarizing aspect of this debate lies in the balance between correcting historical injustices and ensuring that artistic and literary merit remains the primary criterion for recognition and analysis. This tension is exacerbated by the evolving definitions of what constitutes merit and the role that gender plays in shaping perspectives and interpretations.

Furthermore, the portrayal of female characters in literature has been a significant point of contention. Historically, these characters were often written by men and tended to conform to limited and stereotypical roles. The debate intensifies around whether these portrayals were a product of their time and should be understood contextually, or if they perpetuate harmful stereotypes that need to be actively challenged and reformed in modern literature.

This debate provokes strong feelings because it touches on deeper issues of gender equality, historical justice, and cultural identity. It asks fundamental questions about how we value and interpret art and literature and the role of gender in those processes. The discussion reflects a broader societal struggle to reconcile a legacy of gender bias with a growing demand for equality and representation, making it a central, enduring, and often divisive aspect of the discourse surrounding women in art and literature.

Coalition Speech (Progressive Viewpoint)

In support of the active re-evaluation and elevation of women's contributions in art and literature to correct historical imbalances and promote gender equality

Ladies and gentlemen, esteemed judges, and fellow debaters, today we stand at a crossroads in our cultural journey. We are gathered here to address an issue of profound importance: the representation and contributions of women in art and literature. It is with conviction and urgency that I voice the motion, "This house supports the active re-evaluation and elevation of women's contributions in art and literature to correct historical imbalances and promote gender equality."

Imagine, if you will, a world where half the sky is obscured, where the voices of half the population are muted. This is not a scene from a dystopian novel, but a reflection of our historical reality. For centuries, women have been systematically excluded from the artistic and literary fields. They were denied education, professional opportunities, and their rightful place in the pantheon of cultural creators. We have lost countless treasures - ideas, stories, perspectives - all because these voices were silenced by the gates of tradition and prejudice.

But the impact of this exclusion goes beyond just numbers. It has skewed our understanding of the world. Think of the female characters in classic literature, often confined to roles of passivity or moral purity, written not by women but through the eyes of men. These characters, lacking depth and authenticity, have shaped societal perceptions and reinforced gender biases. The question, then, is not just about representation but about the truth in representation.

This brings me to the heart of our argument: the need for corrective measures to achieve gender equality in these realms. Let's consider the untold stories of women artists and writers, overshadowed throughout history. Rediscovering and elevating these figures is not just an act of restoration; it's a step towards rewriting a more truthful and inclusive cultural narrative. Modern representation needs to reflect the societal change we are witnessing - a shift towards diversity and equality. Our art and literature must mirror the world we live in, a world where women's voices are heard loud and clear.

And what of the benefits of this diversity? Ladies and gentlemen, diversity in perspectives is not a mere embellishment; it is the core of artistic and literary richness. When we open the doors to diverse voices, we enrich the tapestry of our cultural heritage. We foster creativity, innovation, and a deeper understanding of the human experience. And beyond the realms of art and literature, this inclusivity has profound educational and societal implications. It teaches our children the values of equality and respect. It inspires young girls and boys alike to dream bigger, to see themselves not just as passive recipients of culture but as active creators.

In conclusion, the motion before us is not just a call for change in the art and literature sectors. It is a call for a cultural renaissance, a renaissance of equality, diversity, and truth. This house firmly believes in the necessity of this change, not just as an act of reparation for the past but as a beacon of hope for the future. Let us therefore unite in supporting the motion, for in elevating women's contributions in art and literature, we elevate humanity itself. Thank you.

Opposition Speech (Conservative Viewpoint)

Opposed to the prioritization of gender over artistic merit in the evaluation of art and literature and supports maintaining a neutral, merit-based approach

Ladies and gentlemen, esteemed colleagues, we gather here today to debate a matter of utmost importance and relevance: the representation and contributions of women in art and literature. While the intentions of the coalition's motion are noble, it is with a deep sense of responsibility and conviction that I present our opposition: "This house opposes the prioritization of gender over artistic merit in the evaluation of art and literature and supports maintaining a neutral, merit-based approach."

Let us embark on a journey through history and reason, to understand why artistic merit must remain the cornerstone of our evaluation. Art and literature are not just reflections of society; they are its pillars, built on the foundation of creative freedom and excellence. Throughout history, the measure of a work's worth has been its quality, impact, and ability to transcend time and space. This is not a subjective perspective but a truth acknowledged universally.

Consider the legacy of great female artists and writers who have graced our history. Their work was celebrated not merely because they were women, but because of their undeniable talent and artistic brilliance. To prioritize gender over merit would not only undermine their achievements but also set a dangerous precedent. It risks compromising the very standards that have elevated art and literature to their esteemed status.

Moreover, the interpretation of art and literature demands a contextual understanding. It is anachronistic and unjust to judge historical works solely through the lens of contemporary values. These works were created in their own unique contexts, and to understand their true meaning and value, we must appreciate them within those contexts. By doing so, we honor the integrity of the art and the artist alike.

As we move forward in time, we naturally see the evolution of society reflected in our art and literature. This evolution should be organic, not forced or mandated. When we allow artists and writers the freedom to create without constraints, their work becomes a genuine reflection of the times. An enforced focus on gender representation risks stifling this natural creative expression and the evolution it brings.

Furthermore, we must be cautious of overcorrecting historical imbalances to the point of reverse discrimination. Art and literature should not be battlegrounds for social agendas. Prioritizing gender over merit could inadvertently lead to a situation where individuals are selected for their gender, rather than their talent. This not only undermines the principle of fairness but also devalues the contributions of those selected under such criteria.

In conclusion, while we recognize the need for equality and representation in all fields, this must not come at the cost of artistic integrity and merit. Our opposition stands firmly on the belief that the true value of art and literature lies in their ability to transcend social constructs, including gender. Let us celebrate and elevate works of art and literature for their merit, for their ability to speak to us across ages and cultures, and for the sheer brilliance of their creation. Thank you.

Challenging questions

10 questions from the coalition to the opposition:

1. How do you reconcile the merit-based approach with the historical context where women were denied the same opportunities as men to develop and showcase their artistic talents?
2. In what ways can a purely merit-based system ensure that the biases and prejudices of those evaluating the art and literature do not overshadow the actual merit of the work?
3. If artistic merit is subjective and often influenced by societal norms, how can we ensure that this subjectivity does not continue to marginalize women's contributions?
4. How does the opposition propose to address the historical lack of visibility and recognition of female artists and writers in a system that continues to prioritize merit, which has traditionally favored men?
5. Can the opposition provide examples where focusing solely on merit has successfully led to equal representation and acknowledgment of both genders in art and literature?
6. How do you respond to the argument that a merit-based approach has historically been influenced by gender biases,

and what measures can be implemented to prevent this from continuing?

7. What is the opposition's stance on the role of art and literature in shaping societal perceptions, especially regarding gender, and how does a merit-based approach account for this?

8. How would the opposition address the criticism that a merit-based system, in its current form, often fails to recognize the diverse forms of expression and narratives that women bring to art and literature?

9. In what ways can a merit-based approach be adapted to acknowledge and correct the underrepresentation of women in art and literature without compromising on quality?

10. How does the opposition propose to balance the need for historical context in evaluating art and literature with the contemporary movement towards gender equality and representation?

10 questions from the opposition to the coalition:

1. How does the coalition plan to objectively measure the historical imbalances they aim to correct without introducing subjective biases into the process?

2. What criteria would be used to determine which female artists and writers are elevated, and how will this avoid creating a new form of bias or exclusion?

3. How can the coalition ensure that the re-evaluation of women's contributions does not inadvertently lead to a tokenistic representation of female artists and writers?

4. In what ways can the coalition guarantee that the quality of art and literature is not compromised in the process of elevating women's contributions?

5. How does the coalition propose to deal with the potential issue of reverse discrimination, where male artists and writers might feel marginalized?

6. Can the coalition provide historical examples where similar corrective measures have successfully achieved the intended balance without compromising artistic merit?

7. How does the coalition plan to reconcile the subjective nature of art and literature with the objective goal of correcting historical imbalances?

8. What mechanisms will be put in place to ensure that the elevation of women's contributions does not become a temporary trend but leads to lasting change?

9. How does the coalition address concerns that their approach might lead to an overcorrection, where the focus shifts from artistic quality to fulfilling gender-based criteria?

10. In what ways will the coalition ensure that their efforts to promote gender equality in art and literature do not inadvertently enforce a new set of restrictive norms or standards?

Potential solutions to reconcile the two parties

In the spirited debate on the representation and contributions of women in art and literature, finding common ground between the coalition and the opposition is not only desirable but essential for progress. The pathway to this middle ground begins with the **acknowledgment of historical imbalances**. Both parties can agree that history has not always been fair in its recognition of female artists and writers. This shared understanding paves the way for the first solution: the establishment of **joint committees** comprising members from both sides to identify and address historical disparities. This committee could work towards **curating exhibitions and publications** that showcase underrepresented female artists and writers, balancing quality with representation.

Building on this, a potential compromise lies in the **education sector**. Both sides can collaborate on developing a more inclusive curriculum that incorporates a broader range of artists and writers, including underrepresented women, ensuring a **balanced representation** without compromising on artistic merit. This educational initiative would cultivate a deeper appreciation and understanding of diverse contributions from an early age.

Another solution lies in the **sponsorship and funding** of artistic and literary projects. Both groups can advocate for funding bodies to allocate resources equally to projects by both male and female artists and writers. This approach encourages a **meritocratic and gender-inclusive system** of funding, where quality is paramount, but opportunities are equally accessible.

Moreover, the coalition and opposition can agree on the importance of **mentoring and networking programs** for emerging artists and writers, irrespective of gender. Such programs could focus on skill development, ensuring that all artists and writers, especially those from underrepresented groups, receive the support they need to excel.

In the realm of literary and artistic criticism, a **diverse panel of critics** from various backgrounds and ideologies could be formed. This panel's role would be to review and critique works in a manner that is fair and comprehensive, taking into account both **artistic merit and the importance of diverse perspectives**.

Further, both sides can support the idea of **commissioning new works** that explore and celebrate the contributions of women in art and literature. These commissions would not only elevate women's voices but also ensure that these works meet high artistic standards.

In the digital age, an innovative solution could be the creation of an **online platform** dedicated to women in art and literature. This platform would serve as a repository and showcase for their work, providing global access and recognition, yet maintaining a **high standard for inclusion**.

Another area of potential compromise involves **research and publication**. Joint efforts could be made to support academic research into the contributions of women in these fields, leading to publications that highlight their work, again balancing representation with merit.

The coalition and opposition might also agree on the importance of **regular reviews and assessments** of progress in these areas. These reviews would ensure that the steps taken are effectively addressing the concerns of both sides, maintaining a balance between elevating women's contributions and upholding artistic merit.

Lastly, a shared commitment to **ongoing dialogue and collaboration** between both sides could be established. This commitment would ensure that the conversation continues, evolving with changing social contexts and maintaining a balance that honors both artistic merit and fair representation.

In weaving these solutions into the fabric of our cultural institutions, we create a narrative of progress and inclusivity, one that respects the values of both the coalition and the opposition, and more importantly, enriches our collective artistic and literary heritage.

Identifying Viewpoints

Identify the Progressive Viewpoint:

What: The progressive viewpoint in this debate is the advocacy for re-evaluating and elevating the work of female artists and writers, and the push for actively challenging and reforming the portrayal of female characters in literature to correct historical imbalances and stereotypes.

Why: This aspect is considered progressive because it aligns with key tenets of progressive ideologies, such as advocating for social change and reform. It emphasizes the need to address and rectify historical injustices and underrepresentation of women. The viewpoint supports the idea of evolving cultural and literary narratives to be more inclusive and representative of women's experiences and contributions. This perspective advocates for a transformation in how female artists and characters are perceived, moving away from traditional norms and towards a more egalitarian and contemporary understanding of women's roles in art and literature.

Identify the Conservative Viewpoint:

What: The conservative viewpoint in this debate is the argument for a 'neutral' approach in judging art and literature, where works are assessed irrespective of the creator's gender, and the idea that historical portrayals of female characters should be understood and appreciated within their historical context.

Why: This aspect is considered conservative as it aligns with the preservation of traditional norms and an emphasis on historical context. It advocates for maintaining established standards in evaluating art and literature, focusing on artistic merit as the primary criterion, rather than the gender of the creator. This viewpoint tends to resist changes to the established canon and prefers to view historical works through the lens of their time, suggesting that they should be understood and appreciated within the context of the period they were created. This approach emphasizes the importance of tradition and continuity in cultural and literary narratives, adhering to long-standing norms and resisting significant changes to how art and literature are interpreted and valued.

Political Analysis

Progressive/Liberal (Left) Viewpoints:

In support of elevating women's contributions (progressive aspect): A significant segment of the left likely views the elevation of female artists and writers, as well as the reformation of female character portrayals in literature, positively. This group advocates for gender equality, inclusivity, and addressing historical injustices in the cultural narrative. They may also support intersectional approaches that consider other aspects of identity such as race, class, and sexual orientation. Estimated percentage of this group: 70%.

In support of neutral approach in art and literature judgement (conservative aspect): A smaller segment of the left might support a more neutral approach, focusing on artistic merit without emphasizing the creator's gender. This portion could argue that while historical context is important, it should not override the quality of art and literature. They might also believe in the importance of preserving historical works as cultural artifacts. Estimated percentage for this viewpoint: 30%.

Conservative/Republican (Right) Viewpoints:

In support of elevating women's contributions (progressive aspect): Within the conservative camp, there might be a subset that recognizes the need to address historical underrepresentation of women in art and literature. This group, while maintaining conservative values, could advocate for more inclusivity and recognition of women's contributions. However, they might emphasize this change within the framework of existing traditions. Estimated percentage representation: 30%.

In support of neutral approach in art and literature judgement (conservative aspect): The majority of conservatives may favor maintaining a neutral approach to judging art and literature, focusing on the artistic merit and historical context. They likely value traditional perspectives on cultural and literary works and may view changes to the established canon with skepticism. This group prefers continuity and the preservation of historical works in their original context. Estimated percentage for this group: 70%.

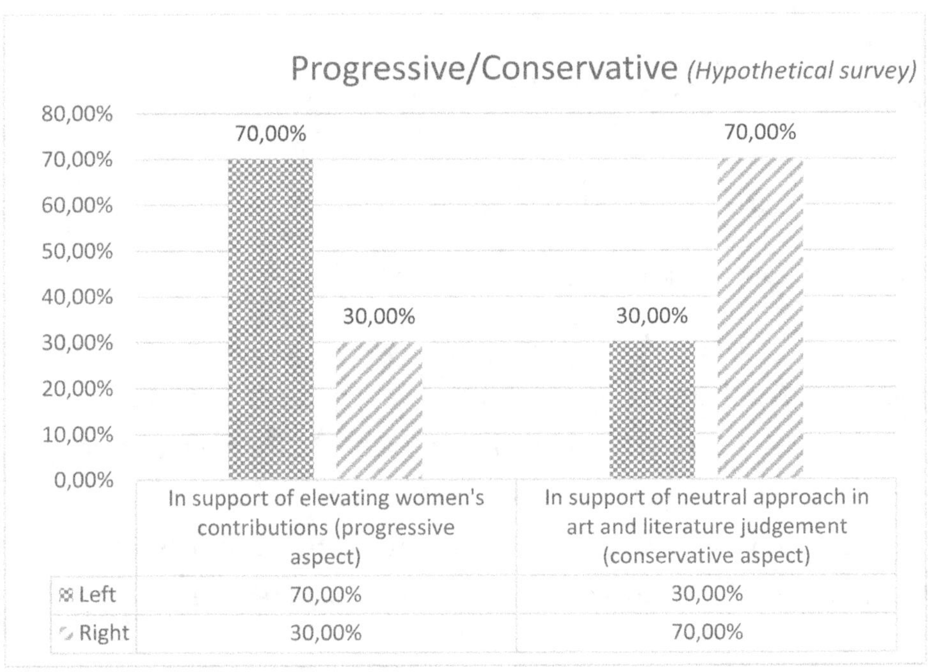

	In support of elevating women's contributions (progressive aspect)	In support of neutral approach in art and literature judgement (conservative aspect)
Left	70,00%	30,00%
Right	30,00%	70,00%

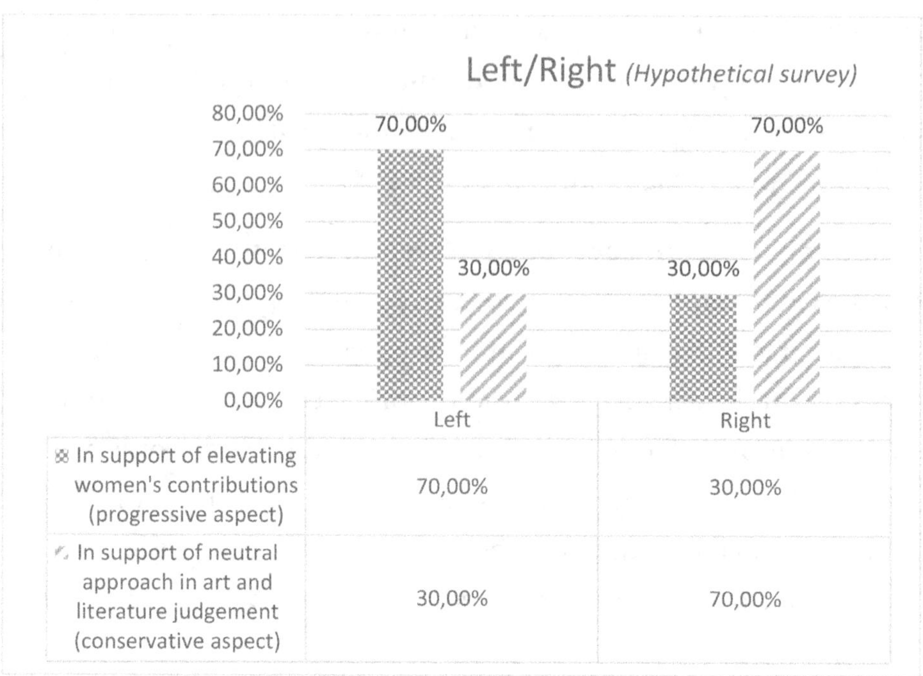

	Left	Right
In support of elevating women's contributions (progressive aspect)	70,00%	30,00%
In support of neutral approach in art and literature judgement (conservative aspect)	30,00%	70,00%

Recommended Resources

Ninth Street Women[34] by Mary Gabriel

Coalition/Opposition Breakdown: 80/20

This book presents the stories of five women artists who challenged the patriarchal norms in the world of twentieth-century abstract painting. Its focus on women artists fighting for recognition in a male-dominated field aligns significantly with the coalition's position. However, it also delves into their artistic merits, offering a slight nod to the opposition's merit-based perspective.

---

[34] https://amzn.to/46M4uj9

<u>*Stop Telling Women to Smile*</u>[35] by Tatyana Fazlalizadeh

Coalition/Opposition Breakdown: 90/10

Fazlalizadeh's book deals with street harassment and includes powerful murals against it, emphasizing women's experiences and voices in society. While it strongly aligns with the coalition's viewpoint on elevating women's experiences, there's a minimal acknowledgment of the opposition's merit-based argument, as the artistic merit of the murals is inherent but not the book's primary focus.

<u>*Broad Strokes*</u>[36] by Bridget Quinn

Coalition/Opposition Breakdown: 70/30

"Broad Strokes" shifts the historical perspective to focus on major women artists, aligning with the coalition's aim of elevating women's contributions. However, by highlighting the artistic merits of these women, it also respects the opposition's stance on merit, thus offering a more balanced view.

<u>*The Art of Tasha Tudor*</u>[37] by Harry Davis

Coalition/Opposition Breakdown: 60/40

This book offers an overview of Tasha Tudor's life and work, showcasing her contributions as a children's book author and

---

[35] https://amzn.to/41aYu2e
[36] https://amzn.to/46O4H5e
[37] https://amzn.to/47S6rfu

illustrator. It leans towards the coalition's perspective by highlighting a woman's contribution in a traditionally male-dominated field. However, it also focuses on the artistic merit of her work, giving considerable weight to the opposition's viewpoint.

Augusta Savage[38] by Jeffreen M. Hayes, Kirsten Pai Buick, and Bridget R. Cooks

Coalition/Opposition Breakdown: 75/25

Augusta Savage's story as a sculptor overcoming poverty, racism, and sexual discrimination aligns more with the coalition's perspective. The book focuses on her struggles and achievements as a woman artist, which is in line with the coalition's aim to elevate women's contributions. However, it also showcases her artistic works, thereby acknowledging the opposition's emphasis on artistic merit.

Artemisia Gentileschi[39] by Jonathan Jones

Coalition/Opposition Breakdown: 80/20

This book about Artemisia Gentileschi, a significant woman artist of the Baroque age, aligns more with the coalition's view. It focuses on her life story, especially her experiences of gender-based injustice, aligning with the coalition's aim to bring attention to women's

---

[38] https://amzn.to/3GxLiLn
[39] https://amzn.to/3NjqGKK

experiences in art. However, it also discusses her art, which aligns slightly with the opposition's merit-based stance.

Their Eyes Were Watching God[40] by Zora Neale Hurston

Coalition/Opposition Breakdown: 70/30

Zora Neale Hurston's novel, while being a significant literary work in its own right, also tells an important story about race, oppression, and femininity. It aligns more with the coalition's perspective by highlighting a female narrative in literature, but since it's also recognized for its literary merit, it offers some alignment with the opposition's viewpoint.

Homegoing[41] by Yaa Gyasi

Coalition/Opposition Breakdown: 65/35

Yaa Gyasi's "Homegoing" is a narrative that spans generations, focusing on themes like slavery, family, and identity from a female perspective. It leans towards the coalition's view by bringing forth women's narratives in literature. Yet, its acclaim as a literary work also gives due credit to the opposition's merit-based argument.

---

[40] https://amzn.to/3NiNnyF
[41] https://amzn.to/3RwdUuN

<u>*Things I Don't Want to Know*</u>[42] by Deborah Levy

Coalition/Opposition Breakdown: 60/40

This memoir reflects on Deborah Levy's life as a female writer, resonating more with the coalition's aim to highlight women's experiences in literature. However, it also delves into the quality of her writing and her reflections on the craft itself, which aligns partially with the opposition's emphasis on merit.

<u>*Things I Don't Want to Know*</u>[42] by Deborah Levy

---

[42] https://amzn.to/4a7I6ng

Chapter 8: Cultural Practices and Women's Rights

Explore controversial cultural practices (like foot binding, veiling) from a historical perspective, discussing their origins, implications, and the modern debate around cultural relativism and women's rights.

At the heart of the debate around controversial cultural practices such as foot binding and veiling, and their relation to women's rights, lies the complex and often contentious interplay between cultural tradition and individual rights. This intersection forms the epicenter of a profound global dialogue, striking at the core of how societies understand, respect, and sometimes challenge deeply rooted customs in the face of evolving views on human rights, particularly women's rights.

The origins of these practices, rooted in historical and cultural contexts, are often symbolic and were perceived as essential elements of societal norms and personal identity. For instance, foot binding in ancient China was seen as a symbol of beauty and status, while veiling in various cultures has been interpreted as a mark of modesty or religious adherence. These practices, deeply ingrained in the social fabric, were passed down generations, creating a sense of continuity and belonging.

However, as global awareness of women's rights grew, these traditions came under scrutiny. Critics argue that such practices, regardless of their cultural roots, often perpetuate gender inequality and can result in physical and psychological harm. This perspective emphasizes the importance of individual autonomy and the universal application of human rights, challenging the idea that cultural practices should be immune to criticism or change.

On the other side of the debate, proponents of cultural relativism contend that understanding and preserving cultural practices is vital for the diversity and richness of global cultures. They argue that external judgments on these practices are often laden with biases and a lack of understanding of the cultural context, leading to oversimplification and disrespect of cultural heritage.

This dichotomy provokes strong debate due to its fundamental nature, questioning the boundaries of cultural preservation and the universality of human rights. The debate is not just about the practices themselves, but what they represent in a larger context of cultural identity, historical continuity, and the evolving understanding of women's roles and rights in society. It challenges individuals and societies to ponder: to what extent should cultural practices be upheld in the face of changing global norms, and how can a balance be struck between respecting cultural heritage and ensuring the rights and well-being of individuals, particularly women, within those cultures?

This narrative encapsulates the essence of the debate, highlighting the delicate balancing act between cultural relativism and the universality of human rights, a central issue that continues to divide opinions and provoke profound reflection and discussion in the modern world.

Coalition Speech (Progressive Viewpoint)

In support of the re-evaluation and reform of cultural traditions that compromise women's rights and individual freedoms

Ladies and gentlemen of the esteemed audience,

Today, we gather under the auspices of a profound debate, a debate that strikes at the very heart of what it means to be a part of the human community. "This house supports the re-evaluation and reform of cultural traditions that compromise women's rights and individual freedoms." This statement, bold in its simplicity, is a beacon of progress, a call for us to look beyond the veil of tradition and into the dawn of a future where equality and human rights are not just ideals but realities for all.

At the core of our argument lies the unwavering belief in human rights and gender equality. Picture, if you will, a young girl, her feet bound, not just by cloth but by centuries of a tradition that sees her not as an individual, but as a symbol. Foot binding, a practice that once flourished in ancient China, serves as a stark reminder of how cultural practices can result in the violation of fundamental human rights. We stand in an era where bodily autonomy and the right to health are recognized as universal rights. Can we then, in good conscience, turn a blind eye to practices that rob individuals of these basic freedoms?

Moving beyond the individual, we see the broader strokes of gender discrimination painted across cultures. These practices are not mere rituals; they are manifestations of a deeper, more insidious form of inequality. They are the chains that have held back half the world's population. It is not just about the physical pain; it is about what these practices represent - a world where women's rights are secondary to cultural norms.

But let us not be mistaken. Our call for change is not a rejection of culture. Cultures are living, breathing entities, capable of growth and evolution. History is replete with examples of societies that have recognized the harmful aspects of certain traditions and have courageously moved past them. The abandonment of foot binding in China is not a tale of cultural loss; it is a story of cultural awakening, a testament to the resilience and adaptability of cultural identity.

In the grand tapestry of global human interaction, we find ourselves at a crossroads. The era of globalization has brought with it a universal recognition of certain inalienable rights. The principles enshrined in international human rights treaties do not recognize geographical or cultural boundaries. They speak a universal language - the language of humanity.

Yet, we understand the delicacy of the balance between respecting cultural diversity and upholding human rights. This is not a call for cultural homogenization; it is a plea for cultural harmonization - a world where cultural traditions flourish without infringing upon the rights and dignities of individuals.

Ladies and gentlemen, as we stand here today, let us ask ourselves - what kind of world do we want to leave behind? A world shackled by the rigid chains of unexamined traditions, or a world that soars on the wings of freedom, equality, and respect for individual rights?

In conclusion, let us remember that progress is not the enemy of culture. Rather, it is the ally of a vibrant, dynamic, and equitable society. This motion is not just a statement; it is a clarion call for us to march towards a future where every individual, irrespective of gender or cultural background, can live with dignity, free from the shadows of oppressive traditions.

Thank you.

Opposition Speech (Conservative Viewpoint)

Opposed to the imposition of modern values on historical cultural traditions, advocating for their preservation and respect

Ladies and gentlemen,

In the tapestry of human civilization, each thread of culture, woven over millennia, forms a pattern rich in tradition, history, and identity. Today, we stand to oppose the notion of imposing modern values on these intricate designs of human heritage. Our stance is not a defense of stagnation but a celebration of diversity and a plea for respect and understanding.

Firstly, let us address the sovereignty and diversity of cultures. In every corner of our world, unique traditions have blossomed — from the veils that dance in desert winds to the intricate patterns formed by foot binding in ancient China. These practices are more than mere relics; they are living embodiments of history, memory, and identity. To impose modern values on these traditions is not progress; it is cultural imperialism in a new guise. History teaches us the perils of such imposition – cultural erosion, loss of diversity, and the diminishing of the rich tapestry that makes our world. Anthropological studies echo this, highlighting the vitality that diverse cultural expressions bring to our global community.

Turning to our second point, we must consider the historical context and continuity of these practices. The threads of tradition are not spun in a day; they are the cumulative work of generations, carrying stories, wisdom, and identity. The practice of veiling, for instance, spans centuries, adapting and evolving within its cultural sphere. It is not merely a piece of cloth but a symbol woven into the fabric of societies. Similarly, foot binding, now ceased, was a complex symbol of beauty and status in its time. To disregard these practices as mere remnants of a bygone era is to ignore the continuum of human history and the role these traditions play in shaping cultural identity.

Lastly, we must embrace ethical relativism and cultural understanding. In a world eager to universalize, we forget the importance of seeing through the lens of others. What is deemed right or wrong, progressive or regressive, should not be dictated by a singular worldview. Philosophers of ethics have long argued for the understanding of moral standards within their cultural context. Change, if it must occur, should stem from within, through intra-cultural dialogue and understanding. The changes we admire in history – the cessation of foot binding, the evolving roles of women in various societies – were not the results of external pressures but internal reflection and gradual transformation.

In conclusion, this house must stand against the imposition of a monolithic set of values upon the diverse cultural practices that make our world. Our aim should not be to erase the lines of difference but to read the stories they tell. Let us not be the generation that undoes the rich, intricate patterns of our shared human heritage in the name of a misguided notion of progress. Instead, let us be the custodians of diversity, the champions of respect, and the advocates for true understanding.

Thank you.

Challenging questions

10 questions from the coalition to the opposition:

1. How do you reconcile the preservation of cultural traditions with the rights of individuals who may be harmed or oppressed by these practices?
2. In cases where cultural traditions inherently discriminate against women, how can we justify their continuation in the name of cultural diversity?
3. What mechanisms would you propose to ensure that the preservation of cultural traditions does not infringe upon the universal human rights of women?
4. How can a society distinguish between cultural practices that are valuable heritage and those that are harmful relics of the past?

5. Can the principle of cultural relativism be sustainably upheld in a globalized world where universal human rights are increasingly prioritized?

6. How does your argument address the potential for cultural traditions to evolve and adapt in response to changing societal values and norms?

7. In what ways can a community internally challenge and reform harmful cultural practices while still maintaining its cultural identity?

8. How do you propose to handle situations where members of a culture themselves call for the abolition or reform of certain traditional practices?

9. Is there a risk that the argument for cultural preservation might be used to justify practices that are clearly detrimental to the well-being and rights of individuals, particularly women?

10. How do we navigate the fine line between respecting cultural practices and preventing the cultural endorsement of gender inequality and violation of human rights?

10 questions from the opposition to the coalition:

1. How do you propose to differentiate between cultural practices that require reform and those that are essential to cultural identity and heritage?

2. In advocating for the re-evaluation of cultural traditions, how would you ensure that this process is not dominated by a Western-centric perspective?

3. What criteria would you use to determine when a cultural practice is harmful enough to warrant intervention or reform?

4. How can you guarantee that the push for reform does not lead to the erosion or loss of unique cultural identities and traditions?

5. How does the coalition plan to engage with and respect the viewpoints of those within the cultures who wish to maintain their traditions?

6. What measures would be in place to prevent the imposition of external values on societies with different cultural and moral frameworks?

7. How would your approach address the potential backlash or resistance from communities whose traditions are being challenged or changed?

8. Can you provide examples where external intervention in cultural practices has led to positive change without causing cultural or social disruption?

9. How does the coalition's stance account for the complexity and diversity of opinions within cultures regarding their own traditions?

10. How would the coalition ensure that the process of re-evaluating and reforming cultural practices is inclusive and sensitive to the needs and voices of all stakeholders, particularly those from the cultures in question?

Potential solutions to reconcile the two parties

In the pursuit of harmonizing the perspectives of both the coalition advocating for the re-evaluation of cultural practices and the opposition emphasizing the preservation of traditions, we find ourselves navigating a delicate balance. The key lies in finding solutions that honor the essence of both viewpoints, creating a middle path that upholds human rights while respecting cultural diversity.

The journey begins with the establishment of a multicultural advisory panel, consisting of experts, anthropologists, human rights activists, and representatives from the cultures in question. This panel's role is crucial in providing a nuanced understanding of each practice, ensuring that both the cultural significance and the potential human rights implications are thoroughly considered.

Building upon this, we find our second solution in the promotion of internal dialogue within communities. Encouraging conversations about their traditions allows communities to reflect on their practices, considering both their cultural heritage and the evolving global human rights discourse. This approach respects the sovereignty of cultures while gently nudging them towards introspection and possible self-initiated reform.

Another key solution is the implementation of educational programs that focus on human rights, gender equality, and cultural sensitivity. Education can play a transformative role, not by dictating changes but by empowering individuals with knowledge and awareness, enabling them to make informed choices about their traditions.

A contextual approach to cultural practices forms the next solution. Rather than a blanket judgment or endorsement of practices, each case should be evaluated on its own merits, considering the specific cultural, historical, and social context. This approach avoids oversimplification and respects the complexity of cultural traditions.

Facilitating access to alternative practices is another compromise. Providing options that honor cultural symbols while eliminating harmful elements can be a way to preserve cultural identity without compromising on human rights.

Regular reviews and updates of cultural practices, guided by the multicultural advisory panel, ensure that the practices remain relevant and respectful of evolving societal norms and human rights standards.

The inclusion of voices from within the cultures in international forums and discussions brings a deeper, more authentic understanding of the practices, ensuring that any decisions made are grounded in lived experiences.

A focus on gradual change rather than abrupt abolition of practices allows communities to adapt and evolve at a pace that is respectful of their cultural processes. This slow transition respects the history and identity of the culture while moving towards a more rights-respecting future.

Legal measures, where necessary, should be considered as a last resort, primarily in cases where the practice causes undeniable harm. Even then, these measures should be implemented with cultural sensitivity and in consultation with the communities affected.

Finally, fostering a culture of global cultural exchange and understanding can create an environment where different communities learn from each other, sharing ideas on how to balance tradition with modern human rights standards.

In weaving these solutions together, we create a narrative that neither imposes modern values on historical traditions nor turns a blind eye to the harm some practices may cause. This balanced approach holds the potential to respect the sanctity of cultural diversity while championing the cause of human rights, creating a world that honors both its past and its future.

Identifying Viewpoints

Identify the Progressive Viewpoint:

What: The argument against the continuation of practices like foot binding and veiling, focusing on individual rights and gender equality.

Why: This perspective is considered progressive due to its emphasis on change, social reform, and the modern interpretation of human rights. The progressive viewpoint prioritizes the autonomy of individuals, particularly women, advocating for their right to choose and live free from traditional practices that may be harmful or discriminatory. This stance often involves re-evaluating long-standing cultural practices through a contemporary lens, with a strong focus on advancing equality and justice. The progressive approach typically involves questioning and challenging the status quo, seeking to align cultural practices with modern values of human rights and gender equality. It represents a move towards inclusivity, non-discrimination, and the promotion of universal standards for human well-being, reflecting a broader shift towards globalized norms and the integration of diverse cultural perspectives under the umbrella of universal human rights.

Identify the Conservative Viewpoint:

What: The defense of cultural practices such as foot binding and veiling as integral parts of cultural heritage and identity.

Why: This viewpoint is considered conservative due to its focus on the preservation of tradition and respect for historical context. Conservative ideologies often emphasize the importance of maintaining established norms and values, viewing them as crucial to the continuity and stability of societies. In this context, conservative arguments support the idea that cultural practices are a fundamental part of a community's identity and should be preserved in the face of globalizing influences and changing societal norms. This perspective underscores a respect for the sovereignty of cultures and their right to maintain and practice their traditions. The conservative stance often views external criticism of these practices as a form of cultural imperialism, arguing that each society has the right to determine its own norms and values. This approach places a high value on historical continuity and the role of tradition in shaping community and individual identity, advocating for a cautious approach to change and a deep respect for the cultural legacy.

Political Analysis

Progressive/Liberal (Left) Viewpoints:

In support of progressive aspect (criticism of traditional practices): A significant portion of the left likely views the progressive aspect positively, advocating for change and emphasizing individual rights and gender equality. They may view traditional practices like foot binding and veiling as oppressive and incompatible with modern human rights standards. Estimated Percentage: 70%

In support of conservative aspect (preservation of cultural traditions): A smaller segment of the left might support the conservative aspect, focusing on cultural relativism and the importance of preserving cultural heritage. They might argue that external judgment of these practices can be ethnocentric and that cultural practices have intrinsic value. Estimated Percentage: 30%

Conservative/Republican (Right) Viewpoints:

In support of progressive aspect (criticism of traditional practices): Within the conservative camp, a smaller fraction might align with the progressive aspect, possibly acknowledging the importance of individual rights and the need to re-evaluate certain cultural practices that may harm women. This group may advocate for a more nuanced approach that balances tradition with modern human rights considerations. Estimated Percentage: 20%

In support of conservative aspect (preservation of cultural traditions): The majority of conservatives may favor the conservative aspect, emphasizing the preservation of cultural traditions and viewing them as an essential part of societal identity and continuity. They may argue against what they perceive as undue interference in cultural practices and stress the importance of historical context. Estimated Percentage: 80%

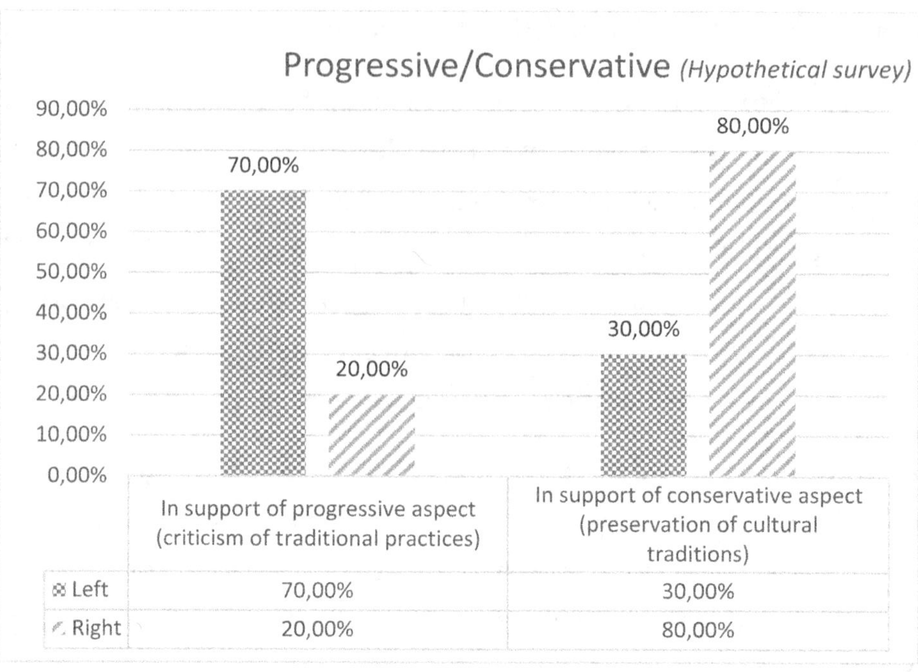

	In support of progressive aspect (criticism of traditional practices)	In support of conservative aspect (preservation of cultural traditions)
Left	70,00%	30,00%
Right	20,00%	80,00%

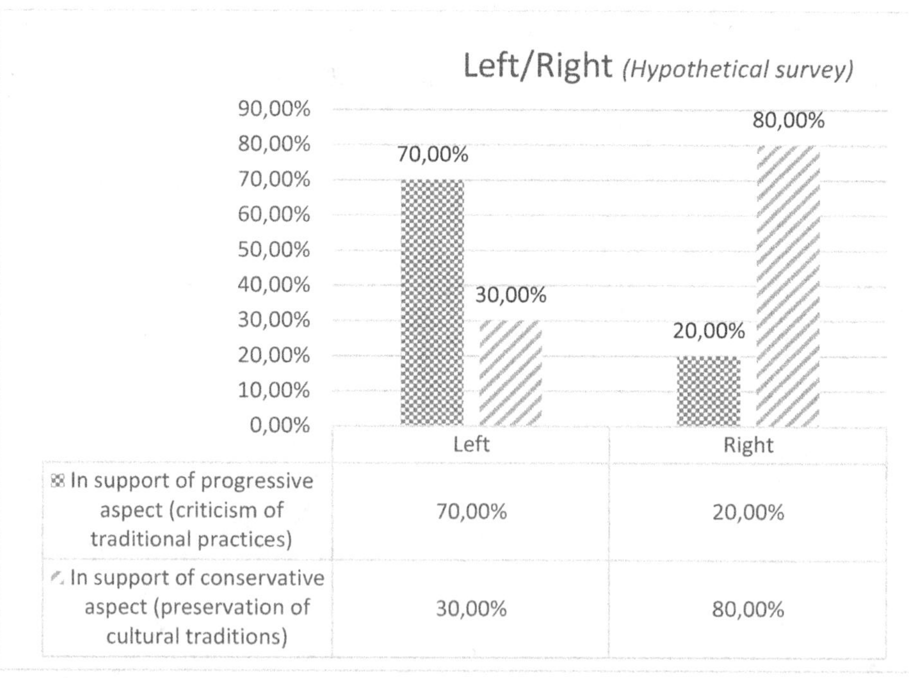

	Left	Right
In support of progressive aspect (criticism of traditional practices)	70,00%	20,00%
In support of conservative aspect (preservation of cultural traditions)	30,00%	80,00%

Recommended Resources

Suffrage: Women's Long Battle for the Vote[43] by Ellen Carol DuBois

Coalition/Opposition Breakdown: 80/20

The book focuses predominantly on the struggle for women's suffrage, aligning closely with the coalition's emphasis on reforming traditions for women's rights. However, it also acknowledges the historical context and complexity of this movement, lending some weight to the opposition's perspective.

The Feminist Promise: 1792 to the Present[44] by Christine Stansell

Coalition/Opposition Breakdown: 70/30

This book presents a historical overview of women's rights, emphasizing individual freedom and collective struggle, aligning more with the coalition's viewpoint. However, it also respects the historical evolution of feminism, thus giving some consideration to the opposition's stance on cultural continuity.

---

[43] https://amzn.to/3uY5e7q
[44] https://amzn.to/46MjKg4

Eighty Years and More: Reminiscences 1815-1897[45] by Elizabeth Cady Stanton

Coalition/Opposition Breakdown: 75/25

Stanton's autobiography discusses her role in the women's rights movement, aligning with the coalition. However, the historical context of her life and work also gives insight into the evolution of cultural practices, which slightly aligns with the opposition's viewpoint.

Vanguard: How Black Women Broke Barriers, Won the Vote, and Insisted on Equality for All[46] by Martha S. Jones

Coalition/Opposition Breakdown: 80/20

This book emphasizes the role of African American women in the women's rights movement, strongly supporting the coalition's stance on reform and equality. It provides a historical context but mainly focuses on challenging and changing traditional norms.

Feminism for the Americas: The Making of an International Human Rights Movement[47] by Katherine M. Marino

Coalition/Opposition Breakdown: 70/30

This book's focus on the international women's rights movement aligns with the coalition's viewpoint of universal human rights and

---

[45] https://amzn.to/3t4tAfr
[46] https://amzn.to/3RzFPdr
[47] https://amzn.to/3TeLK8I

reform. However, it also acknowledges the varied cultural contexts of these movements across the Americas, giving some credence to the opposition's perspective on cultural diversity.

155

Chapter 9: Intersectionality in Women's History

Examine how race, class, and sexuality have intersected with gender in shaping the experiences of women throughout history, highlighting figures from diverse backgrounds.

The most polarizing aspect in the examination of intersectionality in women's history is arguably the differing perspectives on how race, class, and sexuality have synergistically impacted the experiences and struggles of women, compared to the traditional gender-centric view of women's history. This contention arises from the debate on whether intersectionality provides a more nuanced and inclusive understanding of women's history, or whether it complicates and diverts focus from the universal struggles of women as a gender.

On one side of the debate, proponents of intersectionality argue that the traditional narrative of women's history often centers on the experiences of middle-class, heterosexual, white women, thereby marginalizing the unique struggles faced by women of different races, classes, and sexual orientations. They assert that intersectionality is crucial for a comprehensive understanding of women's history, as it acknowledges how factors like race and class shape experiences of oppression and privilege in ways that are not solely defined by gender. This viewpoint highlights historical figures from diverse backgrounds, revealing a richer, more varied tapestry of women's history.

Conversely, critics of this approach argue that emphasizing intersectionality in women's history can lead to a fragmentation of the feminist movement. They worry that it could shift the focus away from shared struggles and goals, leading to divisions within the movement. This perspective often holds that while race, class, and sexuality are important, they should not overshadow the commonalities that unite women in their collective fight against gender-based discrimination and inequality.

The heart of this debate lies in the balance between recognizing the unique challenges faced by different groups of women and maintaining a unified front in the struggle for women's rights. The contention stems from how best to approach the complexities of women's history – whether to view it through a multifaceted lens that considers various intersecting identities, or to focus on a more generalized view of women's shared experiences.

This debate is fueled by strong emotions and deep convictions, as it touches on fundamental questions about identity, solidarity, and the very nature of social movements. It represents a dynamic and evolving conversation that continues to shape the understanding and approach to women's history and rights.

Coalition Speech (Progressive Viewpoint)

In Support of Emphasis on Intersectionality in Women's History

Ladies and gentlemen, esteemed judges, and fellow debaters,

Today, I stand before you to advocate for a motion that is not just a topic of debate, but a call to rewrite history with the ink of truth and inclusivity. This house supports the integration of intersectionality in the study and representation of women's history, recognizing the diverse experiences shaped by race, class, and sexuality. Our history, as we know it, has long been a single narrative - a narrative that, while powerful, has often silenced the voices of those who do not fit into a narrow frame.

Imagine, if you will, a tapestry of history - vibrant, multifaceted, and rich with diverse threads. Each thread represents a story - stories of women of color, LGBTQ+ women, working-class women - whose experiences have been crucial in shaping our society. Yet, for too long, these threads have been overshadowed, overlooked in the grand design of our historical narrative. Today, we argue for their inclusion, for recognizing that their struggles and triumphs are as integral to our history as any.

Firstly, let's talk about representation and inclusivity in women's history. Think of the unsung heroines like Marsha P. Johnson, a black transgender woman who was a pivotal figure in the LGBTQ+ rights movement, or the countless women of color whose activism fueled civil rights movements, yet whose names rarely grace our history books. By broadening our historical perspectives, we not only correct past oversights but also provide a more accurate and complete depiction of our shared human story. This is not just about adding a few names to the chapters of history; it's about reshaping those chapters to reflect a narrative that is more truthful and inclusive.

Moreover, let's consider the undeniable importance of social justice and equality. Intersectionality teaches us that discrimination is not a one-dimensional issue. A black woman's experience in the workplace, for instance, is shaped not just by her gender but also by her race. Policies and movements that fail to recognize these intersecting identities often fall short of addressing the real issues. Promoting equity over equality means understanding that different women face different barriers, and tailoring our solutions to these unique challenges.

Finally, we must acknowledge the imperative of historical accuracy and education. Integrating intersectionality in women's history is not about rewriting history; it's about completing it. It's about ensuring that future generations are educated in a system that recognizes the full spectrum of women's contributions and struggles. It's about ensuring that a young black girl or a queer student sees themselves reflected in the pages of their history textbooks, understands their potential, and recognizes their place in the narrative of our world.

In conclusion, ladies and gentlemen, the motion we present today goes beyond academic debate. It is a motion for change, for justice, and for truth. It is a call to recognize the multi-colored, multi-faceted experiences of all women in our history. By supporting this motion, we are not just advocating for a more inclusive history; we are advocating for a more truthful, just, and equitable world. Thank you.

Opposition Speech (Conservative Viewpoint)

In Support of a Unified, Gender-Centric View of Women's History

Ladies and gentlemen, esteemed members of the house, and fellow participants,

Today, I stand before you not just as a debater, but as a proponent of a vision that has guided the feminist movement through its most successful moments in history. We, the opposition, firmly believe in the strength and necessity of a unified, gender-centric approach to women's history. Our stance is rooted in the understanding that while diversity is important, the focus on shared struggles is what has always driven the movement forward.

Let us first consider the unity and commonality in feminism. History teaches us that the most significant achievements in women's rights have come from a unified front. When women fought for suffrage, it was not their differences that led them to victory, but their shared struggles. The danger of overemphasizing intersectionality lies in the potential fragmentation of our movement. When we begin to divide ourselves, categorizing our struggles into smaller and smaller subsets, we risk diluting the power of our collective voice. Remember, it is our unity, not our differences, that has historically been our greatest strength.

Moving on to the practicality and focus in social movements, we must recognize the efficiency that comes with a unified approach. Clear, focused advocacy and policy-making allow for more effective and impactful changes. Take, for example, the #MeToo movement. Its strength lay in its simplicity – a united stand against sexual harassment, transcending individual identity differences. When we present a singular, powerful message, we are more likely to mobilize support and create substantial change. Overcomplication, on the other hand, can lead to public confusion and diminished support.

Lastly, we must respect the historical continuity and context of the feminist movement. A focus on a unified women's history honors the legacy of our foremothers and the context in which they fought. By preserving their stories in their original, unfragmented form, we pay homage to their struggles and achievements. Furthermore, teaching a more unified version of women's history provides educational clarity, making it easier for future generations to understand and be inspired by the feminist movement.

In conclusion, while we recognize the importance of diversity, we must also acknowledge the power of unity. It is this unity that has always been the cornerstone of our movement. We stand for a feminist movement that is inclusive but not divided, that respects individual struggles but does not lose sight of our collective goals. We oppose the motion not out of disregard for diversity, but out of a deep-seated belief in the strength of our unity.

Thank you.

Challenging questions

10 questions from the coalition to the opposition:

1. How do you propose the feminist movement address the specific challenges faced by women of color, LGBTQ+

women, and women from different socioeconomic backgrounds without integrating intersectionality?

2. In what ways can a unified, gender-centric approach to women's history effectively represent the diverse experiences and struggles of all women?

3. What strategies would you suggest to ensure that the unique issues faced by marginalized groups within the feminist movement are not overshadowed by a broader, unified approach?

4. How can the feminist movement avoid the risk of excluding or marginalizing certain groups of women while focusing primarily on shared struggles?

5. Can you provide historical examples where a unified approach effectively addressed the specific needs and challenges of diverse groups within the women's movement?

6. How does the opposition's stance account for the historical erasure or underrepresentation of certain groups of women in traditional narratives of women's history?

7. If the focus remains on a unified narrative, how do you plan to reconcile and represent the differing priorities and experiences of women from varied cultural, racial, and class backgrounds?

8. How does maintaining a singular focus on gender in women's history align with the contemporary understanding of gender as non-binary and fluid?

9. In advocating for a unified approach, how do you address the critique that this might perpetuate a one-size-fits-all feminism that fails to address systemic inequalities affecting different groups of women?

10. How can the feminist movement ensure it is evolving and adapting to the changing societal landscape without acknowledging and integrating the concept of intersectionality?

10 questions from the opposition to the coalition:

1. How do you ensure that the emphasis on intersectionality does not lead to a fragmented feminist movement, with splintered goals and diluted collective strength?
2. What practical strategies would the coalition propose to effectively integrate and address the diverse intersectional issues without overwhelming the core agenda of the feminist movement?
3. How can the coalition's approach guarantee that the focus on individual group struggles does not overshadow the broader, universal issues faced by all women?
4. Can the coalition provide historical instances where an intersectional focus in women's movements has led to concrete, widespread improvements for women as a whole?
5. How does the coalition plan to maintain a cohesive and united feminist movement while simultaneously addressing the varied and often complex intersectional issues?
6. In advocating for intersectionality, how does the coalition respond to the risk of creating a hierarchy of oppression within the feminist movement, where some struggles are prioritized over others?

7. How does the coalition reconcile the need for a broad, inclusive movement with the potential for intersectionality to lead to endless subdivisions within the feminist agenda?

8. How does the coalition propose to educate and bring awareness about intersectionality in a way that is accessible and relatable to all, regardless of their background or level of understanding?

9. In the coalition's view, how can intersectionality be integrated into women's history without complicating the narrative to the point where it becomes less effective in advocating for women's rights?

10. How does the coalition address concerns that focusing on intersectionality might inadvertently lead to tokenism, where certain groups are included only superficially to meet diversity criteria?

Potential solutions to reconcile the two parties

In the quest for a harmonious resolution to the debate on intersectionality in women's history, it is crucial to explore solutions that address the concerns of both the coalition and the opposition. The first step towards this is the **acknowledgment of the importance of a unified feminist narrative** while also appreciating the nuances brought in by intersectionality. This approach respects the opposition's emphasis on unity and the coalition's push for inclusivity.

A potential compromise lies in the **development of a dual approach to women's history**. This approach would involve the creation of comprehensive historical narratives that highlight shared experiences of women while dedicating specific chapters or sections to intersectional identities. This structure would ensure that no woman's story is left untold, catering to the coalition's desire for inclusivity without losing sight of the common struggles that bind all women, a concern of the opposition.

Another solution could be the **implementation of intersectional training and education within feminist movements**. This training would aim to enlighten members about the various challenges faced by different women, fostering an environment of understanding and empathy. Such training would not only educate members about intersectionality but also reinforce the sense of unity within the movement, bridging a gap between the two viewpoints.

Engaging in **regular dialogues and discussions** among different groups within the feminist movement is also crucial. These dialogues would serve as platforms for women from varied backgrounds to share their experiences and perspectives. By encouraging open communication, both sides can gain a deeper understanding of each other's viewpoints, leading to a more unified approach that still respects individual experiences.

Further, the implementation of **inclusive policy-making processes** within feminist organizations could ensure that all voices are heard and considered. This inclusivity can manifest in the decision-making bodies being representative of diverse groups, thereby ensuring that the policies adopted are reflective of the coalition's emphasis on intersectionality.

The narrative of women's history can also be expanded through **collaborative projects and research endeavors** that focus on underrepresented groups. By pooling resources and expertise, these projects can delve deeper into the histories of marginalized women, bringing their stories to the forefront, a goal of the coalition, while still situating them within the broader context of women's history.

Educational curricula in schools and universities could be designed to include both a unified view of women's history and specific modules on intersectionality. This educational compromise ensures that students gain a well-rounded understanding of women's history, satisfying both sides of the debate.

The use of **modern technology and media** to disseminate information about women's history could play a pivotal role. Creating digital platforms that offer diverse narratives can make history accessible and engaging, allowing for a blend of unified and intersectional perspectives.

Public awareness campaigns that focus on both shared struggles and individual stories can help bridge the gap between the coalition and the opposition. These campaigns can be instrumental in educating the broader public about the complexity and diversity of women's experiences.

Lastly, **periodic reviews and updates to feminist strategies and goals** can ensure that the movement remains relevant and inclusive. This ongoing process would allow both the coalition's and the opposition's viewpoints to be periodically reassessed and integrated into the movement's framework.

Through these solutions, a middle ground that respects and incorporates both the coalition's and opposition's viewpoints can be achieved. This harmonious approach to addressing the debate on intersectionality in women's history not only fosters unity but also ensures that the rich tapestry of women's experiences is fully acknowledged and celebrated.

Identifying Viewpoints

Identify the Progressive Viewpoint:

Aspect: Emphasis on Intersectionality in Women's History

Justification: This viewpoint is considered progressive because it advocates for a change from the traditional, more uniform narrative of women's history. It seeks to modernize the interpretation of women's experiences by acknowledging and emphasizing the diverse and intersecting identities of women, such as race, class, and sexuality. This perspective aligns with progressive ideologies that emphasize social reform, inclusivity, and a more comprehensive understanding of equality. It challenges the status quo by advocating for a broader, more inclusive narrative that recognizes the unique struggles of different groups within the larger category of women.

Identify the Conservative Viewpoint:

Aspect: Focus on a Unified, Gender-Centric View of Women's History

Justification: This aspect is considered conservative as it favors preserving the traditional approach to women's history that focuses primarily on gender-based struggles. It emphasizes the historical context of women's movements and the importance of maintaining a unified front in addressing women's rights. This viewpoint aligns with conservative ideologies that value tradition and caution against the fragmentation of social movements. It advocates for a focus on shared experiences and common goals among women, highlighting the need to maintain established norms and unity within the feminist movement, even if it means less emphasis on the varying experiences of women across different races, classes, and sexual orientations.

Political Analysis

Progressive/Liberal (Left) Viewpoints:

In Support of Emphasis on Intersectionality in Women's History (Progressive Aspect): A significant segment of the left likely views this aspect positively, as it aligns with progressive ideals of inclusivity, social reform, and a broader understanding of equality. This group might believe in acknowledging the unique challenges faced by women of different races, classes, and sexual orientations, and advocating for their representation in the narrative of women's history. Estimated Percentage: 70%

In Support of a Unified, Gender-Centric View of Women's History (Conservative Aspect): A smaller portion of the left might support this aspect, perhaps focusing on the importance of unity in the feminist movement and the risk of fragmentation. They might believe in the value of a shared struggle against gender-based discrimination, even if it means less emphasis on intersectional identities. Estimated Percentage: 30%

Conservative/Republican (Right) Viewpoints:

In Support of Emphasis on Intersectionality in Women's History (Progressive Aspect): There might be a minority within the conservative camp that supports this aspect, possibly acknowledging the importance of addressing the varied experiences of women across different social strata. They might see the value in a more nuanced understanding of women's history that includes intersectional identities. Estimated Percentage: 25%

In Support of a Unified, Gender-Centric View of Women's History (Conservative Aspect): The majority of conservatives likely favor this perspective, valuing tradition and the historical context of women's movements. They might prioritize maintaining a unified front in the feminist movement and focus on common goals and experiences among women, rather than diversifying the narrative. Estimated Percentage: 75%

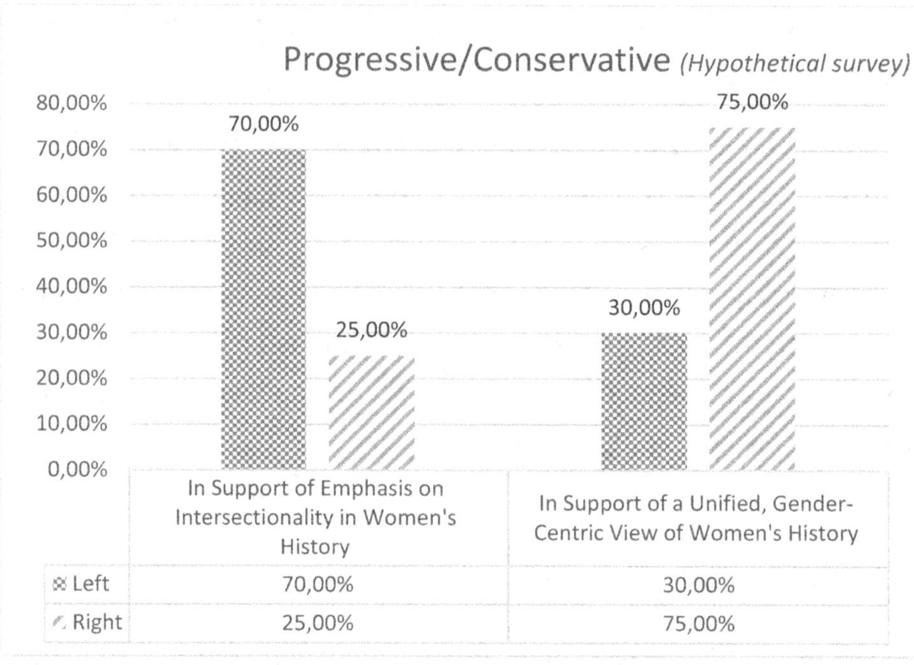

	In Support of Emphasis on Intersectionality in Women's History	In Support of a Unified, Gender-Centric View of Women's History
Left	70,00%	30,00%
Right	25,00%	75,00%

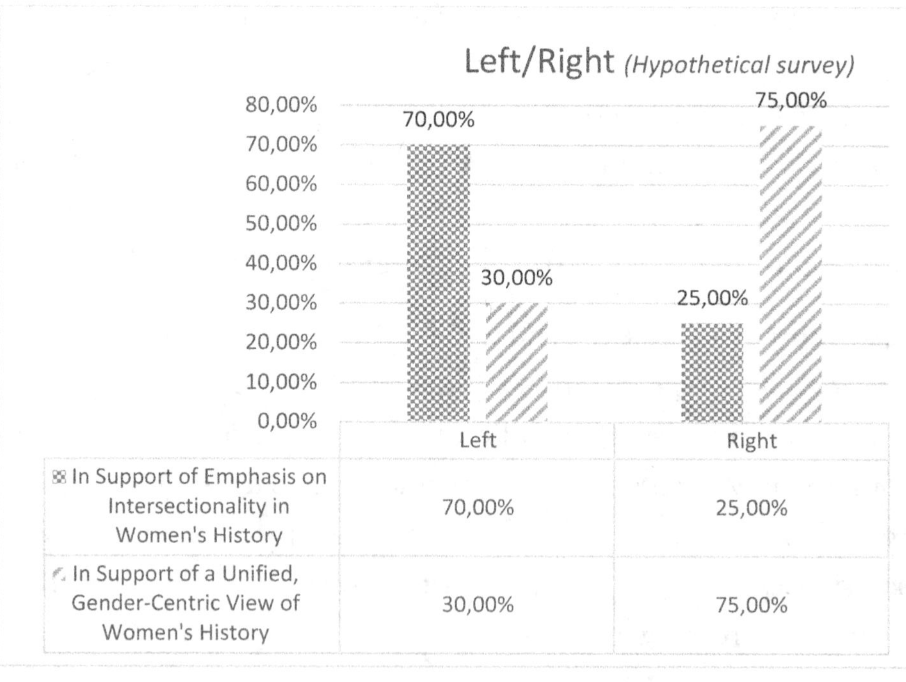

	Left	Right
In Support of Emphasis on Intersectionality in Women's History	70,00%	25,00%
In Support of a Unified, Gender-Centric View of Women's History	30,00%	75,00%

Recommended Resources

No Country Woman[48] by Zoya Patel

Coalition/Opposition Breakdown: 90/10

The memoir focuses on the author's experience as a Fijian-Indian in Australia, emphasizing the intersection of race and cultural identity within feminist contexts, strongly aligning with the coalition's viewpoint on intersectionality. However, there is minimal focus on a unified, gender-centric view, hence the slight tilt towards the coalition's side.

Trans: A Memoir[49] by Juliet Jacques

Coalition/Opposition Breakdown: 100/0

This book strongly aligns with the coalition's viewpoint, as it explores the intersection of gender identity and societal norms, emphasizing the unique challenges faced by a trans woman. It does not address the unified, gender-centric approach favored by the opposition.

---

[48] https://amzn.to/48O06wu
[49] https://amzn.to/3GO3cJO

Women, Race, and Class[50] by Angela Y. Davis

Coalition/Opposition Breakdown: 90/10

Davis's iconic study underscores the intersection of race and gender, particularly focusing on how black women have been historically marginalized in feminist movements, resonating predominantly with the coalition's perspective. The slight allowance for opposition alignment comes from its historical context of unified struggles.

Dark Secrets: After Dreaming[51] by Jeanine Leane

Coalition/Opposition Breakdown: 90/10

Leane's work, centered on the indigenous Australian experience, aligns closely with the coalition's emphasis on intersectionality, particularly racial and colonial aspects. There is a minimal representation of a unified feminist viewpoint.

Don't Call Me Inspirational: A Disabled Feminist Talks Back[52] by Harilyn Rousso

Coalition/Opposition Breakdown: 80/20

Rousso's memoir about overcoming prejudice against disability aligns with the coalition's focus on intersectionality, especially regarding disability and feminism. The 20% alignment with the

---

[50] https://amzn.to/3GKZIrx
[51] http://www.presspress.com.au/leane.html
[52] https://amzn.to/482BJA6

opposition is due to the broader feminist themes that occasionally emerge.

Too Much Lip[53] by Melissa Lucashenko

Coalition/Opposition Breakdown: 80/20

Lucashenko's novel, with its focus on generational trauma and indigenous Australian perspectives, strongly aligns with the coalition's emphasis on intersectionality. The opposition's viewpoint gets some representation in the shared experiences of womanhood.

Hunger: A Memoir of (My) Body[54] by Roxane Gay

Coalition/Opposition Breakdown: 85/15

Gay's memoir, focusing on body image and societal expectations, leans towards the coalition's emphasis on intersectional feminism, particularly in relation to body positivity. The slight tilt towards the opposition's viewpoint comes from the broader themes of women's shared experiences in society.

---

[53] https://amzn.to/3RtwiDe
[54] https://amzn.to/4716cNJ

Sister Outsider: Essays and Speeches[55] by Audre Lorde

Coalition/Opposition Breakdown: 100/0

Lorde's collection of essays and speeches is entirely aligned with the coalition's viewpoint, addressing sexism, racism, homophobia, classism, and ageism, and offering no significant focus on the unified, gender-centric approach of the opposition.

Girl, Woman, Other: A Novel[56] by Bernardine Evaristo

Coalition/Opposition Breakdown: 90/10

Evaristo's novel, exploring the lives of diverse characters, primarily aligns with the coalition's perspective on intersectionality, particularly in terms of race, sexuality, and class. It offers minimal focus on the unified feminist narrative.

Educated: A Memoir[57] by Tara Westover

Coalition/Opposition Breakdown: 60/40

Westover's memoir, while focusing on her personal journey and the transformative power of education, presents a more balanced view. It aligns with the coalition through its exploration of individual struggles against a rigid ideological background, and with the

---

[55] https://amzn.to/3RnemKF
[56] https://amzn.to/3v4GQ4p
[57] https://amzn.to/3v44Apn

opposition in its broader themes of seeking autonomy and education, resonant of universal feminist struggles.

On Intersectionality: Essential Writings[58] by Kimberlé Crenshaw

Coalition/Opposition Breakdown: 100/0

Crenshaw's book, foundational in defining intersectionality, aligns entirely with the coalition's perspective. It explores how gender and race are interconnected, particularly in legal contexts, offering no significant focus on the unified, gender-centric approach of the opposition.

---

[58] https://amzn.to/3tkwuwK

Chapter 10: The Future of Feminism

"Power is not given to you. You have to take it." -
Beyonce

Discuss the direction of contemporary feminism, debating issues like the gender pay gap, reproductive rights, and the impact of movements like #MeToo. Consider the relevance of feminism in addressing the challenges faced by women today.

The most polarizing aspect of contemporary feminism arguably revolves around the concept of gender equality in the workforce, particularly the gender pay gap. This issue strikes at the heart of feminism because it embodies the ongoing struggle for equality in one of society's most fundamental arenas: the workplace. The debate is fueled by differing interpretations of data, disputes over the existence or extent of the pay gap, and varying beliefs about the root causes.

On one side of the debate, advocates argue that the gender pay gap is a clear indicator of systemic sexism. They contend that women, on average, earn less than men for the same work and that this disparity is even more pronounced for women of color. This perspective emphasizes that the pay gap is not just a number but a symbol of the broader inequalities faced by women in the workplace, including issues like glass ceilings, unequal opportunities for advancement, and discrimination.

Opposing viewpoints challenge the methodology used to calculate the pay gap, suggesting that it does not account for differences in career choices, hours worked, or other factors that might legitimately affect earnings. Critics of the mainstream interpretation of the pay gap argue that when these variables are controlled, the gap narrows significantly or even disappears. This side often posits that the focus on the pay gap is misleading and detracts from more nuanced discussions about workplace equality.

The intensity of this debate lies not just in its empirical disagreements but in its deeper implications. It touches on fundamental questions about equality, fairness, and the role of societal structures in perpetuating or mitigating discrimination. It's a conversation that extends beyond numbers and into the realms of social justice, policy-making, and the very definition of equality. This makes the gender pay gap not just a contentious issue, but a symbolic battleground for the broader aims and challenges of contemporary feminism.

Coalition Speech (Progressive Viewpoint)

In Support of Recognizing Systemic Sexism in the Gender Pay Gap

Ladies and gentlemen, esteemed judges, and fellow debaters, today we stand at a pivotal crossroads in our ongoing journey towards gender equality. We are here to affirm that the gender pay gap is not just a disparity in earnings but a glaring symbol of systemic sexism that demands our immediate attention and action.

Picture this: A woman, equally qualified, equally ambitious as her male counterpart, yet, when it comes to her paycheck, she finds a glaring disparity. Why? Is it because she's less capable? Certainly not. It's because our society has entrenched a system where her efforts are undervalued simply because of her gender. This is the harsh reality that women across various sectors face daily. And if she happens to be a woman of color, the disparity is even more pronounced. This is not just an economic issue; it is a moral one.

Let us delve deeper into the roots of this issue. From a young age, girls are often subtly steered towards certain career paths, ones deemed 'appropriate'. This gender stereotyping not only limits their aspirations but also funnels them into lower-paying fields. And when a woman decides to start a family, society expects her to be the primary caregiver, often at the cost of her career growth and earnings. This is not a choice; it is a societal imposition.

The consequences of this systemic inequality are far-reaching. It's not just about less money in the hands of women; it's about their diminished financial independence and security. It perpetuates poverty, especially among single mothers and elderly women. But the impact is not just economic; it's cultural. The pay gap devalues the work traditionally done by women and reinforces damaging stereotypes about their roles and capabilities.

Now, some may argue that the market alone can rectify this imbalance. History, however, tells a different story. Without deliberate policy interventions, progress in closing the gender pay gap has been painstakingly slow. We need only look at countries that have implemented gender equality policies to see the difference proactive measures can make – paid family leave, subsidized childcare, equal pay legislation – these are not just policies; they are statements of what we, as a society, value.

In conclusion, acknowledging and addressing the gender pay gap as a product of systemic sexism is not just about equal pay for equal work. It's about recognizing the inherent value of every woman's contribution to our society. It's about breaking down the barriers that have held back half of our population. It's about building a world where one's gender does not dictate their worth.

So, I urge you, ladies and gentlemen, to stand with us. Stand for justice, stand for equality, stand for a future where no woman has to ask, "Am I being paid less because of my gender?" Thank you.

Opposition Speech (Conservative Viewpoint)

In Support of the Conservative Argument on Gender Pay Gap Methodology

Ladies and gentlemen, esteemed judges, and respected opponents, today I stand before you to unravel a narrative that, while well-intentioned, fails to grasp the nuanced reality of the gender pay gap. We are here to oppose the notion that this gap is predominantly a result of systemic sexism and to propose a more comprehensive understanding of this complex issue.

Let us embark on this journey with a crucial tool: facts. The gender pay gap is often presented as a simple comparison of average earnings between men and women. However, this surface-level analysis omits critical factors like career choices, work hours, and life decisions. Did you know that men and women often gravitate towards different industries and roles, influenced by personal preferences and societal factors? These choices inherently affect earnings. Moreover, men statistically dominate in high-risk, high-paying jobs, which further skews the average.

Furthermore, when we discuss work-life balance, we must recognize that women are more likely to take career breaks for childcare, impacting their long-term earnings. This isn't a flaw of the system; it's a reflection of personal choices and societal norms. We must ask ourselves: are we advocating for equality of opportunity or equality of outcome?

Now, let us delve into the heart of the statistical interpretation. Methodologically, the commonly cited figures of the gender pay gap do not uniformly account for critical variables like hours worked or years of experience. Adjusting for these factors often reveals a dramatically narrowed or even non-existent pay gap. Oversimplifying this data not only misleads policy but also undermines the genuine strides we have made towards gender equality.

Moreover, we must not underestimate the power of individual agency and the free market. By emphasizing personal choice, we respect individual autonomy in career and family decisions. The market, driven by competition and merit, has shown its capability in addressing unjustified wage disparities. There are numerous sectors where the gender pay gap is minimal or even reversed, highlighting the efficacy of market forces.

In conclusion, while the intention behind the coalition's motion is commendable, its foundation is built on a misreading of the landscape. Our approach offers a more balanced, data-driven perspective that respects individual choices and the dynamics of the free market. We believe in equality, but it must be based on a true understanding of the factors at play, not on an oversimplified narrative.

Therefore, I urge you, ladies and gentlemen, to stand with us in seeking a more nuanced and factual understanding of the gender pay gap. Thank you.

Challenging questions

10 questions from the coalition to the opposition:

1. How do you account for the consistent wage gap between men and women in similar positions with comparable experience and education, if not systemic sexism?
2. What explanation can you provide for the fact that women, even in high-paying professions, often earn less than their male counterparts for the same work?
3. How would you address the impact of unconscious bias in hiring and promotion practices, which has been shown to contribute to the gender pay gap?
4. If individual choice is the primary factor in the gender pay gap, how do you explain the societal pressures and stereotypes that influence these choices?

5. Can you elaborate on how market forces alone can rectify wage disparities, given the historical persistence of the gender pay gap despite market competition?

6. How do you propose to support women who face a double burden of professional work and unpaid domestic labor, which affects their career advancement and earning potential?

7. In your argument, you emphasize personal responsibility; how does this viewpoint account for institutional barriers women face in the workplace?

8. What measures would you suggest to ensure that women's choices in career and family life are genuinely free from societal and economic constraints?

9. Can you provide examples of sectors where the gender pay gap is minimal or reversed, and explain how these cases can be generalized to other industries?

10. How do you reconcile the argument of choice with the fact that many women in high-level positions still face a significant pay gap compared to their male counterparts?

10 questions from the opposition to the coalition:

1. How do you explain the variations in the gender pay gap across different countries with similar levels of gender equality, suggesting factors other than systemic sexism?

2. What evidence can you provide to show that the gender pay gap persists when factors like job type, hours worked, and years of experience are controlled for?

3. How does your argument address the fact that in some fields, women are out-earning men, which seems to contradict the notion of a universally systemic gender pay gap?

4. Can you clarify how policy interventions would address non-systemic factors that contribute to the pay gap, such as individual career choices and personal priorities?

5. How do you propose to differentiate between wage disparities caused by systemic sexism and those resulting from personal or biological factors, like maternity leave?

6. What are your thoughts on the potential negative impacts of aggressive wage equalization policies on business autonomy and economic freedom?

7. How would your proposed policies ensure equality of opportunity without enforcing an equality of outcome that might overlook individual preferences and choices?

8. Can you provide examples of where similar policy interventions have effectively and sustainably closed the gender pay gap without unintended economic consequences?

9. How do you respond to the argument that focusing solely on the gender pay gap oversimplifies the complex issue of gender equality in the workplace?

10. What strategies would you suggest to ensure that addressing the gender pay gap doesn't inadvertently disadvantage other groups, maintaining a balance in the workforce?

Potential solutions to reconcile the two parties

In the quest to bridge the gap between the coalition and the opposition in our debate on the gender pay gap, we must embark on a journey of mutual understanding and compromise. The first step in this journey involves **acknowledging the complexity of the issue**. Both parties can agree that the gender pay gap is influenced by a myriad of factors, including societal norms, personal choices, and potential systemic biases. This acknowledgment lays the foundation for a more nuanced discussion.

From this common ground, we can explore the possibility of **developing more sophisticated analytical tools** to assess the gender pay gap. These tools would consider variables like job type, hours worked, and years of experience, providing a more accurate picture that both sides can trust.

Understanding that personal choice plays a significant role in career paths, a solution could involve **enhancing career counseling and educational programs** that encourage all genders to explore a variety of fields, breaking down traditional gender roles. This initiative could be coupled with efforts to **promote flexible working conditions** that cater to the needs of parents, caregivers, and others who balance multiple responsibilities, a move likely to be welcomed by both sides.

Another key compromise lies in the **promotion of transparency in pay**. Companies could be encouraged or incentivized to make their pay scales public, a measure that would provide concrete data for analysis and help identify unjustified pay disparities.

For the coalition's concern regarding systemic issues, a practical step could be the **introduction of targeted policies in sectors with the most significant disparities**. These policies could be piloted as case studies, with their impacts carefully monitored and evaluated, providing a model for potential wider application.

Addressing concerns about economic freedom and business autonomy, it would be beneficial to **encourage voluntary business-led initiatives**. These could include internal audits of pay and advancement opportunities, mentorship programs, and diversity and inclusion training.

The opposition's emphasis on individual agency can be respected through the **promotion of entrepreneurship and skill development programs** for women, equipping them with tools to thrive in competitive markets.

In the spirit of understanding the full spectrum of the issue, both sides could support **comprehensive research initiatives** that delve into the societal and psychological factors influencing career choices and work-life balance decisions.

For the coalition's aim of policy intervention, a balanced approach could involve **advocating for family-friendly policies**, such as subsidized childcare and parental leave, which benefit all workers and contribute to a more equitable workplace.

Finally, we come to the need for **ongoing dialogue and collaboration** between various stakeholders – governments, businesses, advocacy groups, and employees. Regular forums for discussion would ensure that all perspectives are heard and that the solutions evolve with changing societal and economic landscapes.

Through these compromises and solutions, we weave a narrative of cooperation and mutual respect, aiming not just to win a debate but to pave the way for a more equitable and understanding society.

Identifying Viewpoints

Identify the Progressive Viewpoint:

Aspect: The argument that the gender pay gap is a significant indicator of systemic sexism.

Justification: This aspect is considered progressive as it advocates for societal change and challenges the status quo. The progressive viewpoint here emphasizes the need for social reform to achieve gender equality, particularly in the workforce. It focuses on modern interpretations of data to highlight ongoing inequalities and calls for proactive measures to address these disparities. This aligns with progressive ideologies that prioritize social justice, equity, and the transformation of existing systems to accommodate and promote equal opportunities for all, regardless of gender.

Identify the Conservative Viewpoint:

Aspect: The argument challenging the methodology behind the gender pay gap, suggesting that it is not indicative of systemic sexism but rather a result of different choices and circumstances.

Justification: This aspect is considered conservative as it emphasizes the importance of traditional statistical analysis and the interpretation of data within existing societal structures. The conservative viewpoint in this debate typically focuses on individual choice and responsibility, suggesting that differences in pay are a result of personal decisions rather than systemic inequality. This aligns with conservative ideologies that value the preservation of established norms and practices, cautioning against rapid or sweeping societal changes based on what they view as potentially flawed interpretations of data or issues.

Political Analysis

Progressive/Liberal (Left) Viewpoints:

In Support of Recognizing Systemic Sexism in the Gender Pay Gap: This segment of the left views the gender pay gap as a clear manifestation of ongoing gender-based discrimination and inequality. They advocate for policy reforms and greater societal awareness to address this issue. Estimated Percentage: 70%. This group likely forms the majority of the progressive/left viewpoint, as they align closely with core feminist principles emphasizing social reform and equality.

In Support of the Conservative Argument on Gender Pay Gap Methodology: Description: A smaller segment within the left might support the conservative aspect, focusing on the need for more nuanced data analysis. They may believe that addressing the pay gap effectively requires a thorough understanding of its underlying causes, including personal choice and economic factors. Estimated

Percentage: 30%. This group represents a more moderate or centrist position within the progressive/left spectrum, emphasizing data-driven approaches over broad systemic critiques.

Conservative/Republican (Right) Viewpoints:

In Support of Recognizing Systemic Sexism in the Gender Pay Gap: A minority within the conservative camp might acknowledge systemic sexism as a factor in the pay gap. They may support certain reforms or acknowledge the need for societal change to address this issue, possibly blending traditional conservative views with some progressive ideas. Estimated Percentage: 20%. This group, while small, represents a part of the conservative spectrum open to cross-ideological ideas, especially those focused on fair economic practices.

In Support of the Conservative Argument on Gender Pay Gap Methodology: The majority of conservatives likely support the stance that the gender pay gap is a result of individual choices and circumstances, not systemic sexism. They emphasize personal responsibility and economic freedom, arguing for a more traditional interpretation of the data. Estimated Percentage: 80%. This group forms the core of the conservative/right viewpoint, aligning with traditional conservative values of individualism and skepticism towards broad systemic critiques.

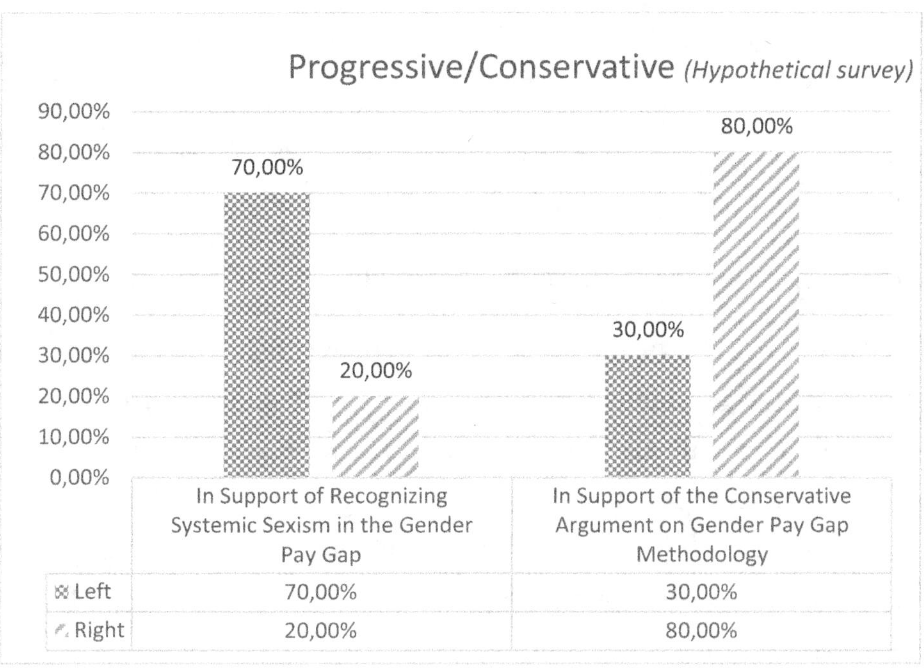

	In Support of Recognizing Systemic Sexism in the Gender Pay Gap	In Support of the Conservative Argument on Gender Pay Gap Methodology
Left	70,00%	30,00%
Right	20,00%	80,00%

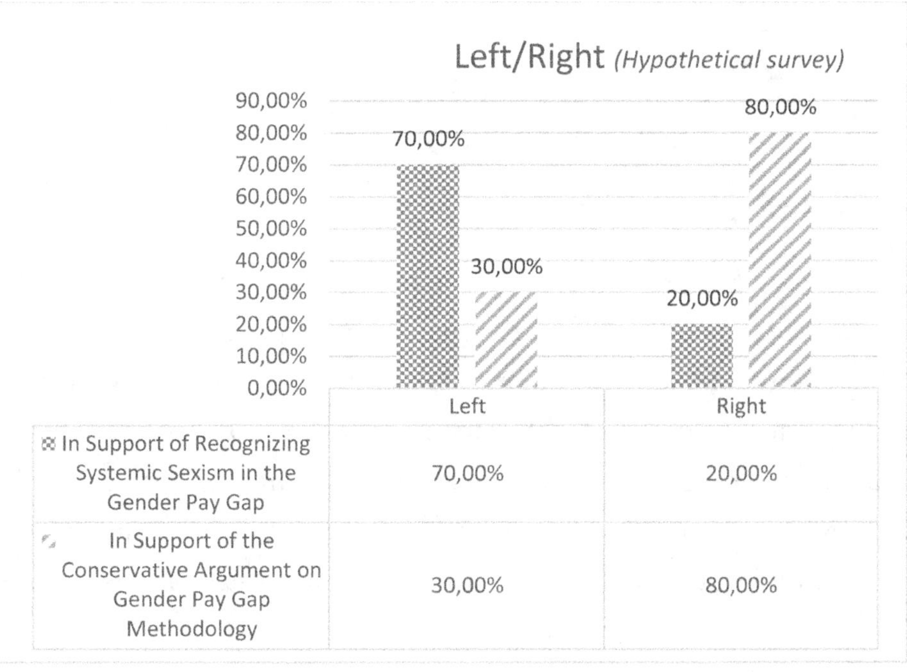

	Left	Right
In Support of Recognizing Systemic Sexism in the Gender Pay Gap	70,00%	20,00%
In Support of the Conservative Argument on Gender Pay Gap Methodology	30,00%	80,00%

Recommended Resources

The Gender Pay Gap: Equal Work, Unequal Pay (In the Headlines)[59] by The New York Times Editorial Staff

Coalition/Opposition Breakdown: 70/30

The content in this book, which includes articles exploring factors that create a gender pay gap and potential solutions, leans more towards the coalition's viewpoint. It acknowledges systemic factors and discusses policy approaches, aligning with progressive ideologies. However, it also delves into economic aspects, giving some weight to the opposition's perspective on individual choice and market dynamics.

Why Men Earn More: The Startling Truth Behind the Pay Gap - and What Women Can Do About It[60] by Dr. Warren Farrell

Coalition/Opposition Breakdown: 20/80

This book focuses on explaining the gender pay gap from the perspective of choices men make in their careers that women don't, which aligns more with the opposition's viewpoint. It suggests that individual choices and differences in career paths significantly influence the pay gap, a key argument of the conservative side. However, it also touches upon what women can do about it, offering a slight nod to the coalition's emphasis on addressing the issue.

---

[59] https://amzn.to/48ga922
[60] https://amzn.to/3RtPqku

The Gender Pay Gap: Understanding the Numbers[61] by Fatma Abdel-Raouf

Coalition/Opposition Breakdown: 60/40

This book tells the story of the gender pay gap by numbers and suggests actions to achieve equity, leaning slightly towards the coalition's viewpoint. It combines statistical analysis with a focus on equity, blending a data-driven approach with progressive calls for action.

The Evolution of the Gender Pay Gap A Comparative Perspective[62] edited by Frances Hamilton & Elisabeth Griffiths

Coalition/Opposition Breakdown: 50/50

This book offers an interdisciplinary research approach to the gender pay gap, presenting a balanced view. It examines both the historical and global impacts of the pay gap, addressing systemic issues (aligning with the coalition) and varied international approaches (resonating with the opposition's emphasis on individual and economic factors).

---

[61] https://amzn.to/48om2TR
[62] https://amzn.to/3RpYyqo

Women vs Capitalism: Why We Can't Have It All in a Free Market Economy[63] by Vicky Pryce

Coalition/Opposition Breakdown: 80/20

Pryce's book argues that the subordination of women causes and is caused by market failure, a view that aligns strongly with the coalition's perspective. It suggests that systemic issues in capitalism affect women's economic status, aligning with progressive ideologies, but also acknowledges the role of market dynamics, giving some room for the opposition's viewpoint.

Invisible Women: Data Bias in a World Designed for Men[64] by Caroline Criado Perez

Coalition/Opposition Breakdown: 90/10

Perez's book focuses on how women's contributions and experiences are often overlooked due to data bias, aligning closely with the coalition's perspective. It highlights systemic issues and the need for more inclusive data practices, which is a core aspect of progressive ideologies.

---

[63] https://amzn.to/4aA65Me
[64] https://amzn.to/48jbcOT

Sex and World Peace[65] by Bonnie Ballif-Spanvill, Chad Emmett, Mary Caprioli & Valerie Hudson

Coalition/Opposition Breakdown: 85/15

This book links the treatment of women to broader societal outcomes, including peace and conflict, aligning predominantly with the coalition's perspective. It underscores the importance of gender equality for societal stability, resonating with progressive arguments about systemic issues.

Delusions of Gender: How Our Minds, Society, and Neurosexism Create Difference[66] by Cordelia Fine

Coalition/Opposition Breakdown: 75/25

Fine's book challenges the notion of inherent gender differences, a viewpoint more in line with the coalition. It argues against biological determinism, supporting the coalition's stance on gender equality and debunking stereotypes, but also delves into scientific and psychological aspects, giving some consideration to the opposition's focus on individual differences.

---

[65] https://amzn.to/3TstRne
[66] https://amzn.to/474BvHB

<u>*Greed, Lust and Gender: A History of Economic Ideas*</u>[67] by Nancy Folbre

Coalition/Opposition Breakdown: 65/35

Folbre's economic history approach to gender roles in the economy aligns more with the coalition's viewpoint. It critiques historical economic theories that have marginalized women's roles, aligning with progressive ideologies, but its historical and economic focus provides some relevance to the opposition's perspective on individual roles in the economy.

<u>*Greed, Lust and Gender: A History of Economic Ideas*</u>[67] by Nancy Folbre

---

[67] https://amzn.to/3TuqbkW

Conclusion

As we conclude our journey through the remarkable roles women have played in history, we leave with a deeper appreciation of their contributions. This book has highlighted not just the achievements but also the challenges women faced across different eras. It's a reminder of the strength and resilience inherent in the female spirit, a call to acknowledge and celebrate the often unsung heroines of our past. As you close these pages, carry with you the inspiration from these stories, and perhaps a new perspective on the impact women have made – and continue to make – in shaping our world.

Index of Recommended Resources

(in alphabetical order)

Books in this series

"Society in Debate™" is a groundbreaking series that delves into the heart of contemporary issues shaping our world. Each volume in this series is dedicated to exploring critical topics that spark passionate discussions and debates across various spheres of society. What sets this series apart is its unique format, a format that brings to life the dynamic and often polarized viewpoints that characterize modern discourse.

At the core of each book in the "Society in Debate™" series is the commitment to presenting arguments from two opposing camps. This approach mirrors the real-world complexity of these issues, where seldom is there a clear-cut right or wrong answer. Readers are invited to explore structured and well-articulated speeches that represent each side of the debate, offering a comprehensive understanding of the arguments and counterarguments.

To further enhance the reader's engagement, each volume includes a series of challenging questions posed by each side. These questions are designed to provoke thought, encourage critical analysis, and allow readers to immerse themselves more deeply in the intricacies of the debates. They serve as a catalyst for reflection, pushing readers to consider their own viewpoints and perhaps even reevaluate their stances on key issues.

Moreover, recognizing the importance of finding common ground, each book in the series explores potential avenues for reconciliation and compromise. This feature is essential, as it acknowledges the complexity of societal debates and the need for solutions that can bridge divided opinions. By presenting these potential solutions, the series underscores the possibility of progress and understanding, even in the face of deep-seated disagreements.

To provide readers with comprehensive insight, each volume also offers a curated list of recommended resources. This feature is particularly valuable for readers who wish to explore the subjects in greater depth.

The "Society in Debate™" series is more than just a collection of books; it is a platform for understanding, discussion, and learning. It invites readers to engage with some of the most pressing issues of our time, providing a space for contemplation and dialogue. As the series continues to grow, it remains committed to enriching public discourse and contributing to a more informed and thoughtful society.

<u>Already published:</u>

<u>Society in Debate: Perspectives on Key Issues</u> by Maggie White

Decriminalization of cannabis - Climate change – Abortion – Immigration - Free speech - Universal basic income - Artificial intelligence - Capital punishment - Internet regulation - Gun control

<u>Society in Debate Vol. 2: Perspectives on Key Issues</u> by Maggie White

Animal Rights - Genetic Engineering - Nuclear Energy - Universal Healthcare - Mandatory vaccination - Cultural appropriation - Capitalism vs. socialism - Age restrictions for voting and other activities - Electoral College - The use of military force and intervention in foreign affairs

Debates on Landmarks & Monuments: A Multifaceted Exploration by Catherine E. Marlowe (Society in Debate Vol. 3)

Preservation vs. Modernization - Cultural Appropriation in Monument Design - Monuments Reflecting Controversial Historical Figures - Impact of Tourism on Landmarks - Representation in Monuments - Economic Cost vs. Cultural Value of Landmarks - Landmarks as Symbols of National Identity - Environmental Impact of Building and Maintaining Landmarks - Public Accessibility vs. Preservation - Digital Reconstruction of Lost Monuments

Modern Faith, Ancient Walls: Navigating the Future of Religious Buildings by Ethan Hawthorne (Society in Debate Vol. 4)

Use of Public Funds - Secular Usage of Religious Spaces - Architectural Dominance in Cityscapes - Representation of Diverse Religions - Sustainable Architecture in Religious Buildings - Modernization vs. Preservation - Commercialization and Tourism - Inclusive vs. Exclusive Architectural Design - Impact of Technology on Religious Architecture - Cultural Appropriation in Architectural Styles

The Ethics of Political Loyalty vs. Constitutional Duty - Media's Role in Shaping Political Narratives - The Historical Precedents of Election Disputes - The Balance of Power Between Executive and Legislative Branches - The Influence of Social Media on Political Mobilization and Radicalization - Comparative Analysis of Democratic Erosion Globally - The Role of Whistleblowers and Insiders in Exposing Governmental Misconduct - The Impact of Nationalistic Movements on Democratic Institutions - The Ethics of Political Violence and Protest - The Accountability of Political Leaders in Democratic Societies